CAVALRY
OF THE AIR

CAVALRY
OF
THE AIR

An Illustrated Introduction to the
Aircraft and Aces of the First World War

Norman S. Leach

DUNDURN
TORONTO

Project Editor: Jennifer McKnight
Copy-Editor: Kat Mototsune
Design: Courtney Horner
Cover Design: Carmen Giraudy
Cover Image: U.S. Library of Congress
Printer: Marquis

Library and Archives Canada Cataloguing in Publication

Leach, Norman, 1963-, author
Cavalry of the air : an illustrated introduction to the aircraft
and aces of the First World War / Norman S. Leach ; foreword by
Colonel John Melbourne.

Includes bibliographical references and index.
Issued in print and electronic formats.
ISBN 978-1-4597-2332-0

1. World War, 1914-1918--Aerial operations. I. Title.

D600.L42 2014   940.4'4   C2014-902136-4
                                        C2014-902137-2

1 2 3 4 5   18 17 16 15 14

We acknowledge the support of the **Canada Council for the Arts** and the **Ontario Arts Council** for our publishing program. We also acknowledge the financial support of the **Government of Canada** through the **Canada Book Fund** and **Livres Canada Books**, and the **Government of Ontario** through the **Ontario Book Publishing Tax Credit** and the **Ontario Media Development Corporation**.

Care has been taken to trace the ownership of copyright material used in this book. The author and the publisher welcome any information enabling them to rectify any references or credits in subsequent editions.
J. Kirk Howard, President

The publisher is not responsible for websites or their content unless they are owned by the publisher.

Printed and bound in Canada.

Visit us at
Dundurn.com
@dundurnpress
Facebook.com/dundurnpress
Pinterest.com/Dundurnpress

Dundurn
3 Church Street, Suite 500
Toronto, Ontario, Canada
M5E 1M2

Books never write themselves. *Cavalry of the Air* happened only because of the support and love of my wife Maritza and my daughters Stephanie and Chelsea.

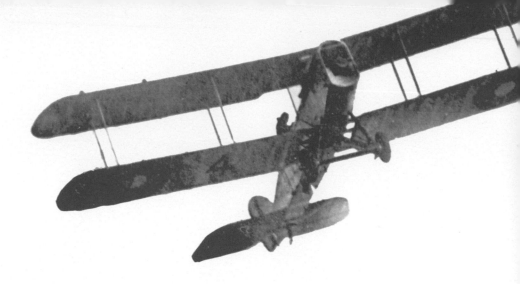

Contents

Foreword

I t is amazing how aviation has progressed over a century — from aircraft of wood and canvas to the modern materials in the high-tech aircraft of today.

The First World War was the first war in which aircraft were used in combat. Observation balloons had already been employed in several wars, including the American Civil War. These platforms were used primarily for artillery spotting. The advancement of aviation, similar to other technical progress, rapidly developed due to war. In 1914, at the outset of the First World War, aircraft were nothing more than gliders with engines. Four years later, they were different — technology had advanced greatly.

The First World War, like any other conflict, was waged with a horrible cost of life. A First World War pilot's life was measured in days, not weeks. This book covers aviation in the First World War and the young men who flew these aircraft.

John E. Melbourne, CD
Honorary Colonel
410 Tactical Fighter (OT) Squadron
Royal Canadian Air Force (RCAF)
"NOCTIVAGA"

Introduction

There is no more iconic image of the First World War than the daring ace flying a rickety machine made of wood and cloth held together with wire. His silk scarf flowing in the wind, the daring aviator challenged his opponent to a fight to the death over the battle-fields of Europe.

Had you been at Baddeck, Nova Scotia, in 1909 — only five years before the start of the First World War — when Alexander Graham Bell's company flew what was hardly more than a kite with a motor, you would not have been able to imagine the advances in aviation that were to come.

For the young cavalry officers looking at the war clouds forming over Europe after 1900, it was increasingly clear that conflict would be very difficult to avoid. In Europe and around the globe, Great Britain and Germany were challenging each other for dominance in a world growing ever smaller through colonization and modernization. New superpowers, including Japan, were flexing their military muscles — defeating great empires on their way to regional power and control. The world was quickly becoming an unstable place in which no one country was clearly the most powerful.

There is a military maxim that generals are always fighting the last war. This is only natural. When generals are young lieutenants they attend military schools where those who fought the last war are the teachers. In every major country, young men look to history for lessons on how to fight the coming war. Unfortunately, in the early twentieth century, history would have little to teach.

In the Boer War (1899–1902) Great Britain and her Dominions faced off against local Dutch settlers, the Boers, determined to keep Great Britain from expanding her territories in South Africa.

Very quickly, the war became one of lightning strikes and rapid retreats by the Boers against rigid British infantry formations. The Boers had early successes that stung the British, and soon the long lines of the infantry were supplemented by hard-riding cavalry and mounted infantry from Great Britain, Canada, and Australia. The horsemen proved perfect for chasing down the Boer raiding parties and for quickly covering the great distances of the South African plains. In the end, Britain's use of mounted troops turned the tide and won the war.

The static trenches and thick, cloying mud of France and Belgium in 1914 could hardly be farther from the plains of South Africa, both in distance and in territory. It didn't take a graduate of a military college to recognize that there would be little role for the cavalry in Europe. While cavalry officers like British Field Marshal General Haig always believed that the great and glorious cavalry charge would make a difference, the men knew better. Soon, dashing cavalry officers were searching for another way to find action and glory. At the same time, forward-thinking generals were searching out new technologies to gain an advantage on the battlefield. The traditions of the cavalry were to become the way of the future.

No technology, ever in history, made the advances aviation did in so short a time. The world moved from Bell's flimsy Silver Dart to German bombers threatening London in well under a decade; from joyriding over farmers' fields to air-to-air combat in less than five years. The airplane became vital to success on the battlefield.

Soon, droves of young men were leaving their horses behind and streaming to aerodromes across Canada, Australia, and Europe. The modern airplane promised freedom from the rigid trench life of the infantry, the freedom of the skies and the glory of personal victory.

The story of First World War aviation is one of man against man, machine against machine. It is a story about daring men holding on to nineteenth-century ideals while their heads were in the clouds of the twentieth century.

There may never again be a time when men and machines were so much in the right place at the right time. What follows celebrates and mourns them all.

ONE

The Wrights, Bell, and Cody

August 27, 1910:
On a flight over New York, John McCurdy sends the first air-to-ground telegraph message ever recorded.

April 27, 1911:
Thousands gather at the exhibition grounds in Edmonton to watch Hugh Robinson make the first airplane flight in Alberta.

May 24, 1912:
Charles Saunders of Vancouver makes the first parachute jump in Canada.

July 6, 1912:
Fred Wells pilots the first seaplane flight in Canada at Hanlan's Point in Toronto Harbour.

July 31, 1913:
Alys Bryant, in Vancouver, is the first woman in Canada to make a solo flight.

American brothers Orville and Wilbur Wright wanted to fly. What's more, the two brothers, bicycle-shop owners from Dayton, Ohio, were convinced that applying scientific principles to the problem would make flight possible.

Building bicycles was a long way from developing a powered, heavier-than-air aircraft that could be controlled in flight. However, the Wright brothers' shop had all the tools, materials, labour, and determination necessary to take on the challenge.

Starting with large, complex kites, the brothers tested the principals of flight. They were not alone. Around the world, inventors were putting their minds to the same problems. Flight was really not the issue — power and control was.

In 1894 Australian Lawrence Hargrave built a rudimentary glider made up of four box kites. Sitting in the sling seat of the "aircraft," Hargrave glided for a total 16 feet (4.9 metres). It was not powered flight, and it was certainly not controlled, but Hargrave's ideas became the basis for many future aircraft designs.

In the United States, Samuel Pierpont Langley, the Secretary of the Smithsonian Institute, published his book *Experiments in Aerodynamics* in 1891. Langley focused on building a pilotless, powered aircraft that would remain stable in flight. The lack of a pilot meant that Langley was not worried about controlling either the direction or altitude of the machine.

On May 6, 1896, Langley was ready to test his aircraft — the Aerodrome No. 5. The plane was loaded onto a catapult that was mounted on a houseboat floating on the Potomac River at Quantico, Virginia. On Langley's order, the catapult was triggered and the pilotless Aerodrome No. 5 flew 3,297 feet (1,005 metres) at an average speed of

25 miles per hour (40 kilometres per hour). Langley had succeeded in completing the first ever heavier-than-air powered flight.

To prove the flight was not a matter of luck, Langley ordered the plane recovered from the river, placed back on the catapult, and launched again. This time it flew 2,300 feet (700 metres).

In November of that year, Alexander Graham Bell, the famed inventor of the telephone and known aviation enthusiast, was on hand when Langley tested his new design — the Aerodrome No. 6. With both inventors intently watching, the airplane flew 4,790 feet (1,460 metres).

But despite the many successes of Hargrave and Langley, controlled, powered, heavier-than-air flight remained elusive.

Back in Dayton, the Wright brothers were experimenting with Hargrave's box kite designs, building even more complex kites — kites that could take off from the ground and sustain flight. As each version was built, modifications were made. Ultimately, it was decided that lightweight spruce frames covered in muslin provided the best chance of success.

Even as they were working on the design of what would eventually become the Wright Flyer (sometimes shortened to the Flyer), Orville and Wilbur knew they were facing a potentially even greater challenge. Somehow they had to design and build a lightweight, internal combustion, gasoline engine that was powerful enough to turn the plane's handmade, wooden propellers fast enough to get the plane airborne. The answer did not come easily.

Wilbur Wright After an Unsuccessful Flight Trial. The early tests of the Wright Flyer did not always go well. This shows Wilbur Wright with the results of an unsuccessful attempt to get airborne at Kitty Hawk, North Carolina, on December 14, 1903.

However, working together with the mechanics in their bicycle shop, the Wright brothers finally made the breakthrough they needed. In late 1903, after years of experimentation and work, the engine was perfected. Made from cast aluminum and fed by a gravity-fed fuel injection system — eliminating the need for a fuel pump and its extra weight — the engine was ready to be mounted to the Flyer.

It was decided to mount the triple-laminated propellers to the Wright Flyer in a *pusher* configuration. Unlike many planes today, in which propellers on the front of the plane pull it through the air, the Flyer's propellers faced backward and pushed the craft through the air.

The final stage was to connect the engine to the propellers. Orville and Wilbur decided to use a method they understood very well. They used two large bicycle chains, looped over sprockets, to transfer the power from the engine to the propellers, making them spin. The Wright Flyer was done and had cost a total of one thousand dollars to build. The only question left was if it would work.

On December 14, 1903, Orville and Wilbur Wright were standing on the sand hills of Kitty Hawk, North Carolina, ready to put the Wright Flyer to the ultimate test. But first the Brothers needed to figure out who was going to fly the airplane. To settle the matter, they tossed a coin — Wilbur won.

The Flyer was positioned facing into the wind, Wilbur at the controls. The engine was started and the craft lifted off the ground — crashing exactly three seconds later. It was powered flight, but it was neither controlled nor sustained.

The Wright Brothers. The Wright brothers, Orville (left) and Wilbur (right), with the 1904 Wright Flyer II at Huffman Prairie.

For the next three days, the brothers repaired the damage caused by the accident. As they worked, they talked about what Wilbur had felt as the plane took off and when it crashed. It had not been an auspicious start, but they were convinced that the Flyer would fly.

On December 17, the Wright Flyer was ready to again challenge gravity. Wilbur had made the first flight; this time it was Orville's turn. The weather had turned bad. The temperature was hovering at near freezing and the wind was blowing at over 25 miles per hour (40 kilometres per hour). No one was sure what would happen.

It turned out the weather actually helped with the flight. As Orville settled in at the controls and applied power, the Flyer seemed to leap into the air. With the headwind helping to carry the craft, the Flyer flew for 12 seconds and travelled 121 feet (37 metres). It had not lasted long, but the Wright brothers had achieved a controlled, powered flight in a heavier-than-air airplane.

Orville and Wilbur had just done what no one else had ever done. They quickly talked about the flight, comparing the experiences of December 14 and December 17. There was no manual for what they were doing. The only way to learn was trial and error — and from each other's experiences.

Wilbur next flew 174 feet (53 metres). Orville then took the Flyer and travelled 200 feet (61 metres) at an altitude of just under 26 feet (8 metres). The final flight of the day was Wilbur's, and he smashed all of their own records. When the Flyer touched down for the last time it had gone 853 feet (260 metres) in 21 seconds.

The Wright Test Flyer at Fort Myer, Virginia, on September 8, 1908. Orville Wright began flying the world's first military flight trials on August 20, 1908, at Fort Myer, Virginia. During the trials the airplane crashed, injuring Orville and killing his passenger, Lieutenant Thomas Selfridge (the first passenger to die in an air crash). Despite this setback, the testing continued and the Wright Flyer surpassed all of the Army's requirements for a military plane. On August 2, 1909, the U.S. Signal Corps took delivery of the world's first military aircraft — Signal Corps Airplane No. 1.

Orville and Wilbur Wright, bicycle-shop owners from Dayton, Ohio, had done it. They had flown an airplane. They had achieved man's dream of flight.

Unfortunately, the world was less than impressed. In January, 1904, on their return to Dayton, the Wright brothers issued a press release, expecting to make headlines. But even their hometown newspaper, the *Dayton Journal*, refused to carry the story. The paper's editor proclaimed that the flight was "too short to be of interest." To the media and public, the Wright's airplane was in the same class as the automobile and the telephone — toys for the rich with no practical purpose. The Wrights still believed the airplane was the way of the future.

Wright Flyer General Specifications

Length: 21 feet (6.43 metres)
Wingspan: 40 feet (12 metres)
Weight: 605 pounds (274 kilograms)
Top speed: 30 mph (48 km/h)
Engine Type: Water-cooled piston engine
Manufacturers: Wright Company, Wright brothers

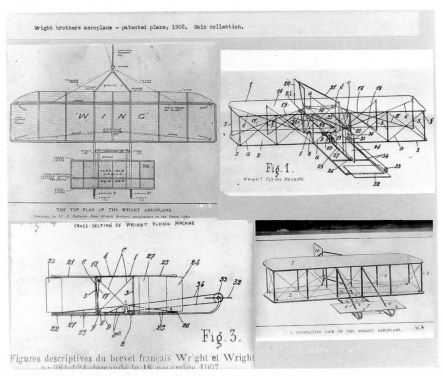

Wright Brothers Patent Plans, 1908. Various plans of the Wright Flyer, including the top plan by W. B. Robinson, as submitted by the Wright brothers to the U.S. Patent Office.
Photo courtesy of the United States Library of Congress, George Grantham Bain Collection.

Death of Charles Stewart Rolls, The Illustrated London News. On the other side of the Atlantic, heavier-than-air flight was also gaining in popularity — and the crashes were growing in number. On July 12, 1910, British aviator (and co-founder of the Rolls-Royce automobile company) Charles Stewart Rolls died in the first fatal air crash in England. The scene at Southbourne, near Bournemouth, in England was captured in the July 16, 1910, edition of The Illustrated London News. Public Domain, The Illustrated London News.

The Silver Dart

As the rest of the world studiously ignored the Wright brothers, famed Scottish-Canadian inventor Dr. Alexander Graham Bell did not. Bell, best known for inventing the practical telephone, was also interested in optical communications (now known as wireless telecommunications), hydrofoils, and aeronautics. When he heard about the flight at Kitty Hawk, Bell believed the Wrights had made an important breakthrough toward practical manned flight.

As one of the founding members of the National Geographic Society, Bell was intrigued by anything new. Further, like the Wright brothers, he believed in the dream of heavier-than-air flight. The result was his establishment in 1891 of the Aerial Experiment Association (AEA) in Hammondsport, New York, to explore the possibilities of that belief. In his pursuit of flight, Bell had not only travelled to Virginia to watch Langley's Aerodrome No. 6 make its first flight in 1896, but also filmed the entire proceedings. He was just as interested in the work being done by the Wright brothers.

By 1908 Bell and the AEA had built and flown three different aircraft, including the June Bug, the winner of the Scientific American Trophy for being "the first aircraft in North America to complete a distance of one mile."

In a search for privacy and inspiration, Bell established a home and laboratory in the tiny village of Baddeck, Nova Scotia, located more than 215 miles (350 kilometres) from the nearest big city, Halifax. The residents of the town showed little interest in what Bell and his team were up to, and the famed inventor found the geography of the area perfect for his work on aeronautics. When the large local bay froze in winter, it made the perfect landing strip.

In early 1909 Bell began moving the assets of the AEA from New York to Baddeck. Included in the move was the AEA's latest aircraft, the Silver Dart (also known as the Aerodrome No. 4).

The Silver Dart was state-of-the-art for 1909. The frame was made from steel tubing, bamboo, tape, wire, and wood; she earned her name from the rubberized, silver-coloured balloon cloth that covered her wings. A V8 engine provided thirty-five horsepower and spun the hand-carved propeller at 1,000 rotations per minute. The design, like those of other early aircraft, did not provide for much control, and the lack of brakes made stopping a challenge.

Bell had the entire plane dismantled and shipped to Nova Scotia.

On February 23, 1909, with the surface of Baddeck Bay frozen solid, pilot and AEA co-founder John McCurdy headed out to the waiting Silver Dart, bundled up against the cold. McCurdy revved up the engine of the Silver Dart and, with the assistance of the ground crew, pointed the plane into the wind.

The Silver Dart travelled down the bay and broke free, lifting off the ground. McCurdy piloted the tiny craft 20 feet (6 metres) above the ground for a half-mile (0.8 kilometres) at an average speed of 40 miles per hour (64 kilometres per hour). It was not a record for distance or speed, but it was the first heavier-than-air flight in the British Empire.

Over the next month, Bell and his team made numerous flights in — and many adjustments to — the Silver Dart. McCurdy once again took the controls of the little plane on March 10, 1909, for its longest flight to date — a circular route of more than 22 miles (35 kilometres).

In August 1909, Bell and McCurdy demonstrated the Silver Dart to the Canadian military in the hope of getting a government contract to build a number of the airplanes. Unfortunately, during the military trials, the Silver Dart crashed and was destroyed. With the Silver Dart gone, Bell dismantled the AEA, but McCurdy and F.W. "Casey" Baldwin (another AEA founding member) purchased the patents for the plane and went on to develop other aircraft.

Portrait of Alexander Graham Bell. Alexander Graham Bell, the famed inventor of the telephone, was responsible for Canada's first heavier-than-air flight. On February 23, 1909, the Silver Dart, an aircraft built by the Aerial Experiment Association (AEA), took off at Baddeck, Nova Scotia, with John McCurdy at the controls. Smithsonian Institution.

Silver Dart General Specifications

Crew: 1
Capacity: 2
Length: 30 feet (9.14 metres)
Wingspan: 40 feet, 1 inch (12.22 metres)
Height: 9 feet, 7 inches (2.92 metres)
Wing area: 563 square feet (52.3 square metres)
Empty weight: 320 pounds (145 kilograms)
Power Plant: 1 × Curtiss air-cooled piston engine, 50 horsepower
(37 kilowatt)

Performance
Maximum speed: 40 mph (64 km/h)
Range: 20 miles (32 kilometres)

The British Army Aeroplane No. 1

Across the Atlantic from Canada's Baddeck, Nova Scotia, American Samuel Franklin Cody was busy building Great Britain's first heavier-than-air craft at the Army Balloon Factory at Farnborough — against some very serious opposition.

In Britain, as in the U.S., few believed that the work being done by the Wright brothers, Bell, and others had any real value. The consensus of most experts was that the future of flight lay in the proven technology of lighter-than-air balloons and airships. Based on this, the British government announced that the only official aircraft to be built in Britain was the Dirigible No. 1, *Nulli Secundus*. Cody, a former Wild West showman (though not the famous Buffalo Bill Cody), was also a well-known early aviator and had originally been hired to work on the *Nulli Secundus*. Working out of the Farnborough Airship Shed in 1906, Cody was responsible for acquiring engines for the airship. By 1907 he was given the responsibility of designing the airship's under-structure and engines.

On October 5, 1907, Cody was onboard the *Nulli Secundus* when she made her inaugural flight from Farnborough to London. At the end of the 3-hour-25-minute flight, the ship's captain tried to land at Buckingham Palace. A strong wind forced the airship down at the Crystal Palace (built in 1861 for the World Exposition and destroyed by fire in 1936). The airship was so badly damaged by the wind that it never flew again.

The crash marked the end of the *Nulli Secundus* but was the beginning of heavier-than-air flight in Britain. Cody, although working on the airship, had believed the future of flight was with the airplane. With the *Nulli Secundus* out of the picture, Cody used his political connections and showman's flair to convince the British government to authorize the construction of a prototype airplane.

Starting with a design similar to the Wright Flyer and the Silver Dart, Cody stretched the wingspan to 52 feet (15 metres). A pair of propellers were driven by a belt connected to a 50 horsepower Antoinette engine (which Cody had managed to salvage from the *Nulli Secundus*).

Finally, in September 1908, the newly christened Cody 1 (also known as the British Army Aeroplane No. 1) was ready to make its first trip down the runway at Farnborough. Cloaked in secrecy, the test run was planned only to see how the plane acted under power. As per the plan, the plane never left the ground, but it ran well. Cody became even more optimistic.

Over the next month Cody and his team worked on fine-tuning the airplane, preparing it for its first public appearance. That day came on October 13, 1908, when Cody, in full view of the media and public, taxied the Cody 1 down the runway at full speed. However, just as in September, Cody did not take the plane airborne. It didn't matter — the day had been a success.

John Rutherford Gordon, Point Cook. A 1916 photo of famed Australian pilot John Rutherford Gordon at the rudimentary controls of an early aircraft. By the time this picture was taken, military aviation technology had far exceeded this craft.

Finally, on October 16, 1908, Cody felt the plane was ready to take to the air. Sitting in the Cody 1 at the end of the runway, Cody revved the engine and released the brake. The tiny plane charged forward and then took to the air. The flight lasted only 1,390 yards (1,271 metres) and ended with Cody damaging the plane's landing gear badly when he put the plane down hard.

Cody wheeled the damaged craft back into the hangar by hand and set to work repairing the damage. It was not until mid-February 1909 that he was ready to fly once again. His timing could not have been worse.

Opponents to heavier-than-air craft had used the Cody 1's crash in October to convince the Aerial Navigation Sub-Committee of the Committee of Imperial Defence to order all funding for the Cody 1 be halted. The Sub-Committee also decreed that the development of airplanes should be best left to the private sector.

Cody, no longer allowed to work on his airplane project, resigned. However, the British government, not wanting to have to store the Cody 1, allowed its builder to take it with him when he left. Just in case they were wrong about aircraft, the British government kept the drawings.

Throughout 1909 Cody continued to fly — and to improve his plane. On July 21, 1909, he flew more than 4 miles (6 kilometres). On August 11, he made the final modifications to the plane, moving the engine behind the pilot. Cody commented, "I find my new position in front of the engine has a much more sensational effect on the nerves than the old position, in fact until last night I never knew I had any nerves. I think, however, I shall get over this slight timidness after a few runs." He did.[1]

On August 13, Cody took his wife along for a three-mile (4.8-kilometre) flight. Mrs. Cody entered the history books as the first woman to fly in an airplane in the United Kingdom.

It was some time before the British again looked at heavier-than-air craft. Other countries in the world had no such reservations.

Cody 1 General Specifications

Crew: 1
Length: 38 feet, 6 inches (11.73 metres)
Wingspan: 52 feet, 4 inches (15.85 metres)
Height: 13 feet (3.96 metres)
Wing area: 640 square feet (59.46 square metres)
Power Plant: 1 × Antoinette, 50 horsepower (37 kilowatts)

Performance
Maximum speed: 65 mph (105 km/h)

TWO

Transition from Cavalry

The iconic white silk scarf worn by early pilots actually had a practical purpose. The flight jackets that kept the pilots warm were made of rough leather. As pilots turned their heads, searching the skies for the enemy, their necks were rubbed raw. The scarves protected against the friction.

In the history of warfare since the 1700s, there have been three kinds of soldiers: the infantryman, who fought on foot; the artilleryman, who worked the cannon; and the cavalry trooper, who fought on horseback. Each had its strengths and weaknesses, but if there was a romantic image in warfare, it was the cavalry.

Up until the end of the First World War, officers were expected to pay for their own uniforms and equipment — which included their horses. The costs could be prohibitive. The result was that the officer corps was comprised of the wealthy and privileged, the only ones who could afford the costs. These wealthy men brought with them a code of *noblesse oblige* — of those to whom great things are given, great things are expected. It was expected that they would live their lives differently from the average working person. Soon, cavalry officers were even separating themselves from their fellow officers in the infantry and artillery.

The Boer War was the last glorious effort for the cavalry. In October 1899, Great Britain declared war on the Afrikaans-speaking Dutch

Cavalry Poster. All the dash and verve that drew young men to the cavalry were captured in this First World War recruiting poster. For all those who hated the idea of slogging through the mud in the infantry, the cavalry was the clear choice.

settlers of the Transvaal Republic and the Orange Free State in South Africa. The Boer War saw some of the most vicious fighting ever.

The response was to bring cavalry to the battle. The environment provided the perfect circumstances — wide open prairies, good footing for horses, and plenty of water and food. Soon, Canada and Australia were assisting the British cavalry by providing some of the best horsemen and horses the colonies had to offer.

The Boers surrendered on May 31, 1902, and were absorbed into the British Empire. The Boer War had been the last great hurrah for the cavalry — it had made the difference in the war, but it would be for the last time.

1870 British Cavalry Officer. A British cavalry trooper in 1870 in full regalia — metal helmet, sword, and saddle. To many in Victorian England, the cavalry troopers and officers cut a very impressive figure.
Author's Collection.

Charger with Shabroque. The cavalry was an elite arm of the army — and an expensive one. Officers were expected to finance their own uniforms, buy their own horses and equipment, and pay for subscriptions (dues) to the Officers' Mess of the Regiment. Officers' horses were often cared for by grooms, who were also paid for by the officer.
Author's Collection.

Boer War Yeomanry. In South Africa the cavalry found it was in its element. The open plains and rolling hills of the country were perfect for both patrolling and fighting. The cavalry started to lighten the load by getting rid of many of the heavy ceremonial helmet and sword, trading them in for rifles and more ammunition.
Lord Strathcona Horse Collection.

Colonel S.B. Steele Commanding Strathcona's Horse, 1900. On the Canadian side of the Atlantic, the cavalry was just as expensive. Famed Canadian mounted policeman and cavalry officer Samuel Benefield Steele would find keeping up with the other officers financially a real challenge. This photo shows Sam heading off to fight in the Boer War in 1900 as the first commanding officer of Strathcona's Horse.

Looming on the horizon was a new future for daring young men. In places as far flung as Canada, the U.S., Great Britain, and Italy, military aircraft were starting to make their appearance.

Almost as soon as the Wright brothers got their first plane in the air, they had approached the U.S. government to offer the craft as a new military tool — though it was hard to imagine the frail Wright Flyer as a weapon in the early days. The U.S. military was skeptical, but agreed to consider the possibility of flight in wartime.

In Britain, when the Aerial Navigation Sub-Committee for the Committee of Imperial Defence recommended heavier-than-air experimentation be ended in 1909, Cody left with his airplane — the army got a set of drawings.

As Britain was shutting down its aircraft program, the military possibilities of heavier-than-air craft were not lost on Alexander Graham Bell and his partner John McCurdy in Canada. Just months after the first flight at Baddeck, McCurdy was presenting the Silver Dart to the Canadian Department of Militia and Defence. On August 2, 1909, two staff officers from the Department watched as McCurdy made three successful flights at Camp Petawawa, north of Ottawa. On the fourth run the plane struck a small rise and crashed. A few days later, McCurdy tried again with the Baddeck No. 1, their second airplane, but it crashed on just its second flight. The Canadian military quickly lost all interest in airplanes until early in 1914.

Troop Canadian Mounted Rifles with 2nd Contingent, South Africa. Despite the practical considerations of fighting the Boers, the cavalry always had time for ceremony. This image of part of the Troop Canadian Mounted Rifles 2nd Contingent photographed with ceremonial lances harks back to an earlier time. Lord Strathcona Horse Collection.

Boer War Mule Cart. Horses (and mules) were not all romance. Caring for horses and other livestock took a great amount of time and energy. For an officer, the work was often taken care of by his batman (soldier who acted as an officer's assistant). For troopers (the non-officers), the work seemed never-ending. Lord Strathcona Horse Collection.

In Italy the military was much more open-minded when it came to airplanes. In 1910 the Italian government established a military flying school at Centocelle near Rome. The first Italian military pilot was Lieutenant Mario Calderara, who had been trained by Wilbur Wright himself. At that time, the Italians were experimenting with the use of aircraft to drop bombs on an enemy force. During the Turko-Italian War in 1911, aircraft were used both for reconnaissance and, on November 1, 1911, to bomb an enemy position.

The skeptics were everywhere. Even as the Italian military was preparing aircraft for real combat, "experts" had their doubts. In 1910 the journal *Scientific American* ran an editorial that read, in part:

> Outside of scouting duties, we are inclined to think that the field of usefulness of the aeroplane will be rather limited. Because of its small carrying capacity, and the necessity for its operating at great altitude, if it is to escape hostile fire, the amount of damage it will do by dropping explosives upon cities, forts, hostile camps, or bodies of troops in the field to say nothing of battleships at sea, will be so limited as to have no material effects on the issues of a campaign.

And yet countries around the world were buying and adapting aircraft for war. The same year as the *Scientific American* article, France bought its first planes and trained 60 pilots. By 1912 the French were practising live bombing runs from giant (for the time) Sikorsky bombers and were trying to perfect a way for aircraft to take off from and land on the deck of a moving ship.

Even the Americans, whose government was committed to non-involvement in foreign wars, were moving to add aircraft to their arsenals. American pioneer aviator Glenn Curtiss was busy building and flying his aircraft with the idea of selling them to the military. On August 20, 1910, he piloted a Curtiss aircraft while Lieutenant James Fickel fired the first shot ever from an airplane — a rifle fired at a ground target 100 feet (30 metres) below.

When U.S. Congress finally appropriated $125,000, on March 31, 1911, to buy aircraft for military use, the U.S. Signal Corps immediately bought five. Less than five weeks later, Lieutenant G.E.M. Kelly became the

Cape Town Camp, 1900. Tents and cannons fill the scene at the Cape Town, South Africa, Camp in 1900.
Lord Strathcona Horse Collection.

first person to die while piloting an aircraft, when he crashed his Curtiss Type IV Model D. But the experiments continued, and in 1912 Captain C.D. Chandler, flying over College Park, Maryland, successfully fired an air-cooled recoilless machine gun from a Wright B Flyer.

Just two years after the *Scientific American* editorial had declared the aircraft of little use in warfare, it was being proven wrong in every major country in the world. Further, waiting in the wings was a new generation of daring cavalrymen, eager to mount a very different kind of steed.

Finally, by 1911 even the British recognized they had made a mistake in not focusing on airplanes, especially for reconnaissance and artillery observation. The Committee of Imperial Defence (which had ordered the cessation of Cody's aircraft project in 1909) in November established another sub-committee to look at the viability of airplanes in warfare. By February 1912, the sub-committee had presented its report and recommended that a flying corps (including naval wing, a military wing, a central flying school, and an aircraft factory) be established. On April 13, 1912, King George V signed a royal warrant establishing the Royal Flying Corps (RFC). By the end of 1912, the RFC had twelve manned balloons and twenty-six airplanes under its command.

Lord Strathcona Horse Lines, South Africa.
A civilian couple visit the horse lines at the Strathcona Horse Camp in South Africa circa 1900.
Lord Strathcona Horse Collection.

THREE

The Beginnings of Air Forces and Air Tactics

Canadian Minister of Militia and Defence Sir Sam Hughes formed the first Canadian military air service — The Canadian Aviation Corps, September 16, 1914.

As the world slowly ground its way toward the First World War, no one could have predicted just how long the war would ultimately go on and how scientific the killing would become. Yet the signs were there. Motor vehicles were replacing horses, machine guns were being mass-produced, and artillery could reach farther with ever-increasing accuracy.

The small and frail aircraft of the Wright brothers, Bell, and Cody seemed ill-suited to combat use, but change was coming to aviation as well. More powerful engines and more robust construction methods meant that military planners were soon looking at the airplane for reconnaissance and bomber duties. The leap to fighter aircraft was just over the horizon.

The Farewell. In 1914 thousands of men from across the Empire answered the call and headed to Europe to fight the Germans. In Canada alone, in August 1914, more than 30,000 men volunteered for overseas service in less than two weeks. Most believed the war would be over by Christmas 1914 — many would not see home again until 1919.

The First World War

When Archduke Franz Ferdinand of Austria was assassinated on June 28, 1914, it triggered a domino effect, with interlocking alliances and treaties drawing countries around the world into war.

Between the Boer War and the First World War the superpowers had aligned themselves in two major groups: the Triple Entente (which would become the Allied Forces), comprised of the United Kingdom (and her Empire), France, and the Russian Empire; and the Central Powers, comprised of Germany, Austro-Hungary, and Italy. Each of the groups had signed binding pledges to support and protect the various nations within their spheres of influence in case of conflict. When a Serb national assassinated the Austrian archduke, the Austro-Hungarian government delivered an ultimatum to the Kingdom of Serbia that would have seen the Serbs essentially concede their sovereignty to the Austro-Hungarian Empire. Naturally, the Serbs refused to comply and the Austro-Hungarians attacked.

The dominos started to fall. As time went on, more and more countries were drawn into the conflict. Italy (having withdrawn from her commitment to the Central Powers), along with Japan and the United States, ultimately joined the Allied Forces; the Ottoman Empire (modern Turkey) and Bulgaria joined the Central Powers. In the end, 70 million men and women served in the various armies, navies, and air forces fighting against each other.

Artillery from the First World War. It is a myth of the First World War that trench warfare was the great killer. In fact, the largest number of men on both sides were killed or maimed not by rifle bullets and hand grenades but by artillery. Hundreds of captured German artillery pieces and machine guns are lined up by the Allies for the media to prove to the folks at home that the good guys were winning. At least that was the idea. *Princess Patricia's Canadian Light Infantry Collection.*

Many believed that the war could not possibly last past Christmas 1914. In fact, the war continued until November 1918, with Allied occupying forces remaining in Germany well past the official end of the war.

The First World War was a war of technology. Unlike the Boer War, combat in Europe saw soldiers facing each other from deep trenches that scarred the landscape of France and Belgium. The new methods of warfare called for new solutions — new and better ways for humans to kill each other.

The Central Powers started the technology race by building thousands of rapid-firing machine guns and highly accurate artillery guns, and then developing poisonous gas. At first the Allies felt that

Tanks. The First World War would see a large number of technical innovations. Tanks, first introduced by the Allies in 1916, were soon a common sight on the battlefield. The behemoths would play pivotal roles at Cambrai and Amiens. *Princess Patricia's Canadian Light Infantry Collection.*

Soldier Trench of the First World War. For the average infantryman — weighted down by 55 pounds (25 kilograms) of equipment — the war was limited to about 10 feet (3 metres) in any direction from his position. As he hunkered down in the trenches and mud of France and Belgium, the romance of war quickly wore thin.
Princess Patricia's Canadian Light Infantry Collection.

machine guns and gas were simply not "gentlemanly" and had no place on the battlefield. However, very soon after the start of hostilities, the Allies were using any new developments that would give them an advantage over the enemy. Horses were replaced by motorized vehicles, heavily armoured tanks made an appearance on the battlefield, and airplanes filled the sky.

Aviation developed, arguably, faster than any other field of technology in the First World War. First used for reconnaissance and surveillance, airplanes were quickly adapted to drop bombs on the enemy. By 1918, when the war ended, airplanes had been modified to do everything from aerial photography to providing air-to-ground support for infantry and tanks.

It was not only machines that changed but men as well. Pilots who, early in the war, learned by experimentation and trial-and-error, were at the end of the war were applying scientific aviation strategies and tactics on the battlefield.

By the time the war ended, four major imperial powers had disappeared — the German, Russian, Austro-Hungarian, and Ottoman Empires. The technology, however, went on. Airplanes were here to stay.

Great Britain

In 1912 the British government, reversing its decision of 1909 that airplanes had no role in future warfare, authorized the establishment of the Royal Flying Corps (RFC). The original plan saw all British aircraft and pilots serving together in a military wing of three squadrons and a naval wing with just one squadron. In 1914 the naval wing became the Royal Naval Air Service (RNAS) and began operating independently from the RFC.

Royal Flying Corps Poster. The battle of the posters. The Royal Flying Corps, at the beginning of First World War, was actively recruiting young men to join the Corps. Money and patriotism were both large draws to the RFC.

When Great Britain declared war on the Central Powers on August 4, 1914, the RFC was commanded by Brigadier-General Sir David Henderson. Only five weeks later, on September 13, 1914, Henderson ordered his aircraft to assist Allied artillery units by spotting the enemy and directing artillery fire, increasing both the accuracy and effectiveness of Allied efforts. While the reconnaissance aircraft proved useful they, like French planes used in the same role, were hampered by not having an effective way to relay information quickly to the ground.

By May 9, 1915, British aircraft were, for the first time, provided with wireless radios. Arriving just in time for the Battle of Aubers Ridge, the wireless sets changed everything.

Planes of the three squadrons of the 1st Wing of the RFC were responsible for patrolling the skies above the battlefield at Aubers Ridge. Before the start of the battle, British planes ensured that German reconnaissance aircraft were not able to observe the British ground preparations.

It was once the battle started that the wireless sets proved invaluable. With secrecy on the ground no longer issue, the British pilots became the eyes of the artillery teams trying to hit enemy guns and infantry. By spotting the enemy artillery and using their new wireless sets, the pilots could communicate with artillery crews and accurately direct shell fire, ultimately saving Allied lives.

LEFT: First World War Observation Balloon. Aviation was not limited to aircraft. Lighter-than-air balloons had been used since the U.S. Civil War, but came into their own in the First World War. With modern communication (circa 1914), the observer could quickly relay changes on the battlefield to the soldiers on the ground. The observation balloons would become ready targets for aircraft, and flying them was dangerous. An American observer, late in the First World War, stands in the unprotected wicker basket of his observation balloon.

RIGHT: British Balloon, Mesopotamia. A British observation balloon prepares for launch some-where in Mesopotamia during the First World War.

Even as the Battle of Aubers Ridge was being fought, the British Army was experimenting with aerial photography in an effort to better track enemy manoeuvres both on the battlefield and behind the lines. At first the experiments were less than successful. Existing cameras simply could not capture images quickly or clearly enough to be of practical use. As time went on, British scientists developed greater speed film, better lenses, and methods to take photos from high altitudes. Working together with aircraft designers, scientists also found ways to make the cameras smaller and more stable. Aircraft, combined with photography, gave war planners a view of the battlefield they had never had before.

The weakness of the reconnaissance planes was that they had little or no defensive armour or guns. They needed fighter aircraft as escorts to protect them — sometimes as many as twelve fighters for one reconnaissance plane. It was a drain on resources but the intelligence proved by the aircraft was worth the cost.

As strategy and tactics improved, the demands on military aviation increased. Early in the war pilots and observers were given bombs to drop by hand on targets of convenience. If it seemed a target could be hit, the crew was encouraged to "give it a go." New airplanes

ABOVE: Burgess-Dunne Float Plane. One of the first aircraft used by the Allied forces in the First World War was the Dunne D.8 Designed and built in 1912 by J.W. Dunne, the plane flew with the Royal Flying Corps (RFC), the U.S. Signal Corps, and the United States Navy. The Canadian Aviation Corps, authorized by the Minister of Militia and Defence Sam Hughes, would exist only for a few months, but the Dunne D.8 was the only plane flown by the Canadian service.

were developed that could travel farther and carry heavier and heavier loads. The result was planes that delivered larger and larger numbers of bombs, not just on tactical targets but on strategic ones as well. To provide defensive capacity, more armour and guns were mounted on the bombers. They still needed fighters to protect them, but the bombers were becoming much more than just a way to deliver bombs.

It was the fighter aircraft that saw the greatest changes, in both design and role. Larger engines delivered more speed and range, better guns provided both defensive and offensive capabilities, better design allowed for more manoeuvrability. As the fighters got more effective, they were used not only to provide escorts but also to provide cover fire for ground troops, to attack enemy bombers and reconnaissance planes, and to engage and destroy enemy fighter aircraft in dogfights high above the battlefield.

German Zeppelin over London. The Germans also used lighter than air craft for both observation and bombing. Here a German Zeppelin sails through the air above London.
Author's Collection.

By 1917 the British government was convinced that aircraft were now a permanent part of the modern battlefield. When General Jan Smuts presented a report on the future of military aviation to the War Council in London in August 1917, he recommended that the RFC and the RNAS be united into one organization, freeing up more planes to serve on the Western Front. Smuts reported that the RNAS, which had been tasked with coastal patrols and naval operations as well as supporting the RFC on the Western Front, was underutilized and that its airplanes and personnel were being wasted.

Following Smut's recommendations the government in London established a new air ministry and ordered the RFC and RNAS to officially merge on April 1, 1918, becoming the new Royal Air Force (RAF), with more than 4,000 combat aircraft and 114,000 personnel serving in 150 squadrons.

Canada

After the disaster at Camp Petawawa, in which John McCurdy and F.W. Baldwin demonstrated the Silver Dart to the Department of Militia and Defence, only to have it crash and break up on landing, the Canadian government had little interest in aviation until the start of the First World War.

When the Governor General declared that Canada was entering the war on August 5, 1914, the mercurial Minister of Militia and Defence Sir Sam Hughes (who had backed the Ross Rifle, the MacAdam shovel, and other disasters of military technology) asked what Canada could do to support military aviation. The Imperial War Council in London suggested that Canada provide six Canadian pilots to the RFC. The challenge for

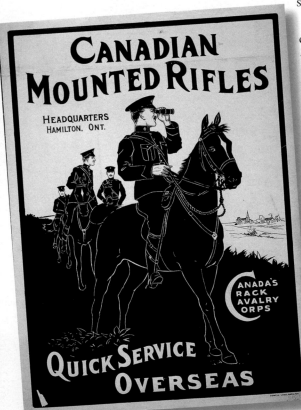

Canadian Mounted Rifles Poster. On the other side, the mounted units were also actively recruiting. The Canadian Mounted Rifles went with the tried and true call to young men in their poster.

5th Regiment Royal Highlanders of Canada and Grenadier Guards. In a scene repeated over and over again in Great Britain, Canada, Australia, and New Zealand, recruits — some with military experience, many with none — trained for the very real conflict in Europe. Here the 5th Regiment Royal Highlanders of Canada and the Grenadier Guards line up at the Canadian training camp at Val Cartier, Quebec.

Hughes was that among 3,000 men in the entire Canadian armed forces there were not six qualified pilots to be found.

Hughes, an ardent Canadian, believed Canada should have its own air force. Not one to be deterred by anything, on September 16, 1914, Hughes ordered the formation of the Canadian Aviation Corps (CAC) and sent it to follow the Canadian Expeditionary Force (CEF) to Europe. Hughes authorized $5,000 to buy one aircraft from the Burgess Company in Massachusetts, and instructed the company to deliver the plane to Val Cartier, Quebec. When the plane arrived on October 1, 1914, the entire CAC — two pilots and one mechanic — was anxiously waiting for it.

The CAC airplane never saw service. After it arrived in England it was put into storage, and soon damp weather conditions damaged the airplane so badly it had to be scrapped. In May 1915, the CAC was disbanded.

Vimy Ridge Canadian Machine Guns. In April 1917 the Canadians took a ridge in Northern France that neither the British nor the French had been able to take. The attack at Vimy Ridge was to be a "sideshow" to the Battle of Arras and was designed simply to draw German defenders away from the main battle. Instead, it forged a nation.

Canadian Cavalry on the way to Vimy. Cavalry head to the Battle of Vimy Ridge. As usual in the First World War, the cavalry were present but seldom used.
Author's Collection.

Hoping to make more aircraft available for the war effort and, at the same time, wanting to spread the costs to others in the Empire, Britain suggested that Canada start recruiting men for a stand-alone Canadian air operation. Having just shut down the CAC and knowing the costs involved in buying and maintaining aircraft, Canada deferred.

However, the Government's reticence to get involved with aircraft did not stop ordinary Canadians from joining the army to learn to fly. Eventually, more than 20,000 Canadians enlisted with either the RFC or the RNAS. Some of those pilots went on to be Canada's greatest aces. By 1917 the RFC established training bases in Canada to directly recruit and train airmen to fight in Europe.

Finally, in the spring of 1918, the Canadian government agreed to establish a force of planes and pilots to fight directly with the Canadian Corps in France. The original plan called for eight squadrons, but the British Air Ministry suggested a much-reduced force of just one fighter squadron and one bomber squadron. Ottawa quickly agreed.

The Canadian Air Force (CAF) was officially formed on September 19, 1918, taking control of the two Canadian squadrons under the command of Lieutenant-Colonel William Avery "Billy" Bishop, Canada's most decorated wartime ace.

Many of the men of the CAF believed that they were to be the vanguard of a new and great Canadian air force with squadrons in both Canada and

Recruits Drilling at Toronto Armoury. Recruits in 1914 practise at the Toronto Armoury. Canada was so unprepared for war, the men would train in their civilian clothes until the logistics caught up to the situation.

Europe. However, in the spring of 1919, the British government stopped funding the CAF, and the Canadian government quickly decided there was no need for an air force at all. The CAF came to an official end on May 30, 1919.[2]

In 1920 the Canadian government again established a Canadian Air Force, but it was primarily focused on civil flying (i.e., search and rescue). It was not until 1924 that Canada would have a true air force.

Australia

In 1911 Australia attended the Imperial Conference in London, as did the other countries of the British Empire. Participants in the conference agreed to make developing military aviation across the Empire a major priority for all attending countries.

On October 22, 1912, the Central Flying School was opened at Point Cook, Victoria, making Australia the only country to live up to its commitment at the Imperial Conference. The Australian Flying Corps (AFC), built on the model established by the RFC, was set up right after the Flying School was opened.

Early in the war the AFC was tasked with supporting Imperial Forces in seizing German-held territory in northeast New Guinea. The AFC planes were packed in crates and shipped to the island. However, by the time they arrived, the Germans had surrendered, so the planes were sent back to Australia, still in their crates.

In the spring of 1915 the AFC was once again sent overseas, this time to Iraq. The aircraft of the AFC, operating as the Mesopotamian Half Flight, were tasked, on May 27, 1915, to support the Indian Army in protecting Iraqi oil fields.

It was the beginning of extended service for the AFC in the First World War. The Australian pilots and airplanes of No. 1, No. 2, No. 3, and No. 4 Squadrons served in Egypt, in Palestine, and on the Western Front. At the same time, the four training squadrons — No. 5, No. 6, No. 7, and No. 8 — provided new pilots and aircrew for the war effort.

Ultimately, 2,694 officers and men served in the Australian Flying Corps, and another 200 Australians served in the RFC and the RNAS. Of those, 175 made the ultimate sacrifice and died in battle.

Moving Equipment Through, Passchendaele. At the Battle of Passchendaele in October 1917, the mud was so thick that men drowned in their holes before even seeing battle. Passchendaele would spell the end of the cavalry. Never again would military commanders seriously consider the mounted arm as a decisive factor in battle. There would be men and horses well into the 1930s, but tanks and airplanes had replaced the arme blanche.
Princess Patricia's Canadian Light Infantry Collection.

Scientific Tactics

Major Edward "Mick" Mannock of the RFC was the godfather of modern air tactics on the Allied side in the First World War. Rather than counting on luck and natural skill in air combat, Mannock applied scientific principles to the task. His cardinal rule, still taught to fighter pilots today: "Always above, seldom on the same level, never underneath." To Mannock, height was the ultimate advantage in air combat.

While governments were establishing air forces, Mannock developed a set of principles that were shared with all new Allied pilots. The goal was to keep them alive longer.

1. Pilots must dive to attack with zest, and must hold their fire until they get within one hundred yards of their target.
2. Achieve surprise by approaching from the East. (From the German side of the front.)
3. Utilize the sun's glare and clouds to achieve surprise.
4. Pilots must keep physically fit by exercise and the moderate use of stimulants.
5. Pilots must sight their guns and practice as much as possible, as targets are normally fleeting.

6. Pilots must practice spotting machines in the air and recognizing them at long range, and every aeroplane is to be treated as an enemy until it is certain it is not.

7. Pilots must learn where the enemy's blind spots are.

8. Scouts must be attacked from above and two-seaters from beneath their tails.

9. Pilots must practice quick turns, as this maneuver is more used than any other in a fight.

10. Pilots must practice judging distances in the air, as these are very deceptive.

11. Decoys must be guarded against — a single enemy is often a decoy — therefore the air above should be searched before attacking.

12. If the day is sunny, machines should be turned with as little bank as possible; otherwise the sun glistening on the wings will give away their presence at a long range.

13. Pilots must keep turning in a dog fight and never fly straight except when firing.

14. Pilots must never, under any circumstances, dive away from an enemy, as he gives his opponent a non-deflection shot — bullets are faster than aeroplanes.

15. Pilots must keep their eye on their watches during patrols, and on the direction and strength of the wind.[3]

Mannock's Rules were so well-respected that young fighter pilots were still being taught them in flight school in the Second World War. Further, a number of British aces of the Second World War publicly commented that, while aircraft technology had changed by 1939, many of Mannock's principles still held true.

Roland, 1914–1915. Even before Passchendaele, it was clear the airplane was to play a major role in the First World War. Never before had a technology advanced so quickly — in peacetime or in war. Very early in the conflict, the German military was flying two Roland airplanes for reconnaissance purposes.

The Great Allied Aces of the First World War

Billy Bishop, the great Canadian ace, played himself in the 1942 movie *Captains of the Clouds*. He appears in a scene in which he presides over the graduation of cadet pilots.

When Bishop arrived in France in 1917, the average life expectancy of a new pilot in that sector was eleven days, and German aces were shooting down British aircraft 5 to 1.

As fascinating as details of the aircraft and tactics of the period might be, the success in air combat on both sides of the air war was built on the skills and daring of the pilots.

The aces (those with five verified kills or more) were the elite of their day, trumpeted in the media and idolized by the general public. On the Allied side, aces were often pulled from the front lines to head recruitment and bond drives in England and their home countries. Across the British Empire, for young men volunteering to serve, flying was the way to fame and glory. The aces were proof of it.

Billy Bishop

Country: Canada
Born: February 8, 1894
Died: September 11, 1956
Number of Victories: 72

Anyone who knew William "Billy" Bishop growing up in Owen Sound, Ontario, knew him as a tough misfit. Billy's father William was a strict disciplinarian who insisted his son wear a suit and tie to school. If that was not enough to make Billy the target of school bullies, he spoke with a lisp, did not participate in team sports (preferring horseback riding and swimming), and, horrors, he liked girls.

The bullying did not last long. Billy quickly gained a reputation as being fearless and for fighting with a ferocity that scared even the biggest boys in his school.

Despite being a poor student, Billy was interested in aviation from his teenage years. When he was fifteen years old, he built an "aircraft" out

Billy Bishop with Plane. Billy Bishop, Canada's greatest ace, is credited with shooting down seventy-two German aircraft, making him the most prolific of the Allied aces. He survived the war and went on to institute the Commonwealth Air Training Program in Canada as Canadian Air Marshal of the Royal Canadian Air Force.
Author's Collection.

of cardboard and wood. Climbing to the top of his family's three-storey house, he settled into the craft and launched himself off the roof. His sister rescued him from the wreckage when he crashed into the ground 25 feet (7.6 metres) below.

Billy's father, worried about his son's future and knowing that his poor grades would never qualify him for university, enrolled the seventeen-year-old in the Royal Military College (RMC) in Kingston, Ontario. Years later Billy commented on his time in Kingston:

> I had never given much thought to being a soldier,
> even after my parents had sent me to the Royal Military
> College (RMC) at Kingston, when I was seventeen
> years of age. I will say for my parents that they had not
> thought much of me as a professional soldier either. But
> they did think, for some reason or other, that a little
> military discipline at the Royal Military College would
> do me a lot of good — and I suppose it did.[4]

Billy's older brother, Worth, had enrolled in RMC and, with some of the highest marks ever seen at the College, was setting a difficult example for Billy to equal. While he did fairly well in the first two years, Billy was caught cheating in May 1914 (he accidently handed in his crib sheets along with the exam paper). He was suspended from the school until a decision could be made on his future; the declaration of war in August 1914 made it all a moot point.

With his riding experience, Billy was naturally assigned to a cavalry unit — the Mississauga Horse, a detachment of the 2nd Canadian Division. Waiting for deployment to Europe, Billy came down with pneumonia and was forced to watch his unit leave without him. Reassigned to the 14th Battalion Canadian Mounted Rifles in London, Ontario, Billy finally made the trip to England and the Shornecliffe Training Area.

Shornecliffe was a quagmire of mud, as the worst rains in decades fell on the area. In July 1915, as Bishop watched, an airplane made a landing in a nearby field so the pilot could get his bearings. Bishop later wrote about the encounter:

> It landed hesitatingly in a nearby field as if scorning
> to brush its wings against so sordid a landscape; then
> away again up into the clean grey mists. How long I
> stood there gazing into the distance I do not know, but
> when I turned to slog my way back through the mud

my mind was made up. I knew there was only one place
to be on such a day — up above the clouds and in the
summer sunshine. I was going into the battle that way. I
was going to meet the enemy in the air.[5]

When speaking to a friend, Bishop was even more emphatic. "It's
clean up there! I'll bet you don't get any mud or horse shit on you up
there. If you die, at least it would be a clean death."[6]

Bishop joined the Royal Flying Corps (RFC) in 1915 but, because
there were no pilot spots available, he became an observer and photographer with No. 21 Squadron, headquartered at Netheravon, U.K. The
squadron was using the R.E.7, a new airplane but one that could fly at
only 70 miles per hour (112 kilometres per hour), making it an easy
target for the much faster German Fokker E.III.

The German anti-aircraft guns were also a threat. Bishop wrote:

It is no child's play to circle above a German battery
observing for half an hour or more, with the machine
tossing about in air, tortured by exploding shells and
black shrapnel puffballs coming nearer and nearer to you
like the ever-extended finger-tips of some giant hand of
death. But it is just part of the never-ceasing war.[7]

Luck was against Bishop in early 1916. He was injured in a truck
accident, knocked unconscious for two days when a piece of an airplane
landed on him, suffered from an infected tooth, and, finally, badly
injured his knee in an airplane crash. In May his commanding officer
sent him to England to rest and recover. His injuries were considered
bad enough that he was sent back to Canada for more care. He could
have stayed home a year, but was back in England in September 1916,
determined to be a pilot.

In November 1916, Bishop received his pilot's wings and was
assigned to No. 37 Squadron, a Home Defence squadron flying the
B.E.2c. He quickly became bored flying over London, searching for airships (he did not see a single airship in more than two months of flying)
and requested a transfer to France. February 1917 found Bishop at No.
60 Squadron near Arras and assigned to the Nieuport 17 fighter aircraft.

After Home Defence duties, being a fighter pilot must have been
a radical change. Just kilometres away was the famed Flying Circus
of Baron Manfred von Richthofen, who was known as the Red Baron.
Considered the most dangerous sector in all of France, the Arras region
provided more than enough opportunities for flying — and fighting.

On March 24, 1917, Bishop and three other pilots engaged three Albatros D.III scouts near Saint-Léger. Bishop was flying the last plane in the Allied formation, a position called *Tail-End Charley*. He focused on one of the enemy planes and chased it almost to the ground — firing all the time. Bishop destroyed the aircraft, making his first kill on his very first flight. He would see seventy-two victories before the war was over.

Bishop was immediately made a flight commander by Squadron Commander Jack Scott, despite the young flyer's very real lack of experience. However, pilots were in short supply and even moderately successful ones were in high demand.

Watching fellow pilots die in combat had a telling effect on Bishop. He returned to the shooting range to perfect his skills — skills he could pass on to the constant stream of replacement pilots arriving at the front. He perfected the deflection shot, or shooting where the enemy plane was going to be. It was not a skill that could be taught — either you had the ability or you didn't.

Bishop received the Military Cross on April 7, 1917, for destroying an enemy observation balloon (a notoriously difficult target, as balloons were well-protected by ground guns and fighter aircraft) and an Albatros

Billy Bishop in Cockpit. Bishop would be a controversial character, despite his having won the Victoria Cross. Historians would question the number of kills he claimed and the actions with which he was credited. Despite this, Bishop would remain a Canadian hero. Author's Collection.

sent to protect it. The next day he took on six Albatros planes by himself, destroying three. By the end of April (only five weeks after first flying in France), Bishop had seventeen kills to his credit. He was the squadron's highest scoring ace, and only Germany's Red Baron had more kills.

Bishop had survived "Bloody April." Others in his squadron had done as well. The loss rate for pilots was 105 percent. Of the original eighteen pilots in 60 Squadron, fifteen were killed; another seven sent as replacements also perished.

Bishop wrote to his fiancée, Margaret: "You have no idea of how bloodthirsty I've become and how much pleasure I get in killing Huns."[8]

Bishop claimed another two kills the same day that British ace Albert Ball was killed, on May 17, 1917. With Ball gone, Bishop was left the highest-scoring ace serving with British forces.

Bishop continued his string of victories, shooting down more reconnaissance planes and enemy fighters. On June 2, 1917, Bishop staged his famous raid on Estourmel Aerodrome (the base of German ace Werner Voss), shooting down a total of three and perhaps four enemy planes. In one two-week period in late May to early June, 1918, Bishop shot down a total of seventeen planes.

By June 19, 1918, the Canadian government was worried that the death of Bishop would have a negative effect on morale at home. He was ordered away from the front and into a command position in Canada.

Not willing to give up easily, Bishop took to the air on his last day at the front and shot down five enemy planes, though he was credited with only three. He finished the war with seventy-two confirmed air victories and the title of highest-scoring British ace.

Billy Bishop's First World War decorations include the Victoria Cross, Distinguished Service Order with Bar, Military Cross, Distinguished Flying Cross, Legion of Honour, Croix de Guerre with Palm, 1914–15 Star, and British War Medal.

Billy Bishop at Military College. Billy Bishop as a very young cadet at military college in Ontario.

Mick Mannock

Country: Ireland
Born: May 24, 1887
Died: July 26, 1918
Number of Victories: 61

Young Edward "Mick" Mannock did not have an easy life. The son of a professional soldier, he lived in Ireland, then Scotland, England, and India (where he contracted an infection that left him temporally blind).

When Mick was twelve years old, his father abandoned the family, forcing the young Mannock to drop out of school and take on a number of menial jobs just to keep his family fed. He eventually became a telephone engineer working with the National Telephone Company and was sent to work on a project in Turkey. While in Turkey, Mick became a committed socialist, attending rallies and speaking often on the benefits of socialism.

In August 1914, after the declaration of war, Mannock tried to get out of Turkey, a country allied with Germany and Austria, as quickly as he could. However, before he found transportation back to England, he was arrested by Turkish police and thrown in jail. Held in solitary confinement and frequently beaten by the guards, Mick made a number of unsuccessful escape attempts. Finally, he was repatriated to England in April 1915, and immediately volunteered for the Royal Army Medical Corps.

Believing that the Medical Corps did not give him the chance to do enough for the war effort, Mick first transferred to the Royal Engineers and then the RFC. Then twenty-nine, Mick

Mick Mannock in Leather Coat. Edward "Mick" Mannock was Irish by birth, but was of English and Scottish extraction. With sixty-one kills, he was the highest scoring British ace. He was known as a highly technical pilot who had an absolute hatred for the enemy. Author's Collection.

had read an article about British ace Albert Ball and was convinced that flying was what he was meant to do.

When he completed training in March 1917, Mick was sent to No. 40 Squadron, stationed at Saint-Omer, France. The working-class socialist had trouble getting along with the pilots of the 40th, many of whom came from wealthy, upper-class families. In a moment of weakness, when challenged that he was not aggressive enough when flying, Mick admitted to being afraid. In the world of First World War pilots, it was a huge mistake. Mick was not alone in fighting with his own inner demons. He had no doubt he was doing the right thing in killing the enemy. He often spoke of how he wished he could kill more but, at the same time, he started to fear his own mortality — particularly of crashing an airplane and being burned alive. In the close confines of an airbase, it was impossible to hide his fitful nights and nightmares.

None of it seemed to bother the solitary Mannock, though. Soon he was accumulating victory after victory — fifteen in total by the end of August, including four enemy aircraft destroyed in one day.

After a brief stay in England, Mannock returned to France with a promotion to Flight Commander of No. 74 Squadron, and his successes continued. Between April 12 and June 17, 1918, he destroyed thirty-six more enemy aircraft.

Mick was highly respected by his men. Many of them, as novice pilots, had Mick flying as their wingman when they made their first kills. Mick felt that, by helping with that first victory, he would build confidence in his men. Carrying it even further, he never claimed any of the kills he assisted with, allowing the novice pilot to take full credit.

He may have been a great pilot, but Mannock was slowly being consumed by the stresses he faced as a fighter pilot. He had developed an overwhelming hatred for the Germans and took great pleasure in seeing them burn to death, despite his fear of

Mannock with Dog, 1917. Mick Mannock would develop a number of phobias during his time in combat. He flew at a time when the lifespan of an Allied pilot was, on average, only eleven days. As time progressed, he obsessed about burning to death in his aircraft — which is exactly how he died. Author's Collection.

burning to death himself. He also began to carry a pistol on every flight. He swore to anyone that would listen that he would prefer shooting himself to being trapped and burned alive in an airplane crash.

Stricken with a case of influenza, Mannock was sent to England to recover in June 1918. He returned to France as Officer Commanding of No. 85 Squadron in July 1918. Soon he had nine more victories to his credit, but his phobias were now fully exposed. He was driven by compulsive tidiness, and more and more he foresaw his own death.

That death came on July 26, 1918, as Mick flew a patrol low over German territory. Flying beside the veteran ace was a novice pilot Lieutenant D.C. Inglis, who was still looking for his first victory. With Mick assisting, Inglis finally found and destroyed a German L.V.G. Victory in hand, the two planes headed for home.

Suddenly, heavy ground fire hit both planes. Mick's S.E.5a was sent crashing to the ground. Inglis returned home and reported that the plane had crashed and burst into flames behind enemy lines.

Mick Mannock's body was found 250 yards (228 metres) from his plane.

Raymond Collishaw

Country: Canada
Born: November 22, 1893
Died: September 28, 1976
Number of Victories: 60

It seemed natural that Raymond Collishaw would join the Royal Canadian Navy. When he dropped out of school at age fifteen, his father had secured him a position on a Canadian Fisheries Protection Boat as a cabin boy.

Quickly promoted to Junior Sailor, young Collishaw was serving onboard the *Alcedo* when it was ordered north of the Arctic Circle to search for the ill-fated Stefansson expedition. They arrived too late to rescue many of the men on the *Karluk,* but Collishaw was awarded the British Polar Ribbon, which he wore with pride (until he found out he was not actually entitled to it and had it removed from all his uniforms).

For the next seven years, Collishaw worked on ships on the west coast of Canada, ultimately reaching the rank of First Officer on the ship *Fispa*.

When war broke out in 1914, Collishaw tried, as was expect with his background and training, to enlist in the Royal Navy, but by 1915 he had received no response whatsoever. Hearing that the Royal Naval Air Service (RNAS) was looking for pilots, he applied in Esquimault, British

Raymond Collishaw in Cockpit. Raymond Collishaw flew with both the Royal Naval Air Service (RNAS) and the Royal Air Force (RAF). His sixty victories made him the RNAS flying ace, second to only to Canadian Billy Bishop among Allied flyers.
Author's Collection.

Columbia, and, after an interview in Ottawa, was accepted.

There was a catch, however. While he was enrolled as a Probationary Flight Sub-Lieutenant, he would become a Lieutenant only when he passed a flight training course — which he had to pay for personally. Undeterred, Collishaw moved to Toronto and tried to enrol in the only flying school in Canada, the Curtiss Flying School. The school was small and did not have enough instructors — and then the weather turned cold.

The RNAS grew impatient waiting for pilots, so Collishaw and others were sent to Halifax to get their basic training before being shipped to England for flight training. In January 1916, his basic training completed, Collishaw sailed for England.

Collishaw finished his training in England in 1916, having completed only eight-and-a-half hours of solo flying and despite the fact that he was still having trouble landing an airplane. New flying certificate in hand, Collishaw joined the RNAS's 3rd Wing in Ochey, France, flying the British Sopwith 1½ Strutter. His first victory came over Obendorf, Germany, during a raid on the Mauser Arms Works.

More than eighty Allied aircraft took part in the mission to bomb the arms manufacturer. When the Nieuport 11 fighters that were flying escort duty were forced to turn back due to low fuel reserves, the remaining planes were intercepted by German Albatros D.IIs, including one flown by Ernst Udet (later one of Germany's most prolific aces), who claimed his first victory that day.

Fighting off the attackers, Collishaw and his gunner singled out a German plane flown by another future ace, Ludwig Hanstein. Both the gunner and Collishaw were able to hit the enemy plane with machine-gun fire. Hanstein landed his plane and lived to fight another day. Collishaw, as he nursed his damaged craft the 200 miles (322 kilometres) home, could think only about his first victory.

Soon the Canadian pilot was flying sortie after sortie, making kill after kill. Collishaw also set another pattern — having his aircraft shot out from under him and walking away. On December 27, 1916, while returning from a raid on a steel works at Dillingen, Collishaw's plane was damaged and he crashed just inside French lines at Nancy. The plane was a wreck but the ace walked away.

In January 1917, he had an even more dramatic escape. While flying a Sopwith 1½ Strutter to a new base, Collishaw was attacked by six Albatros D.IIs. A violent battle followed, with Collishaw shooting down two of them. However, one of the German bullets shattered the Canadian's flying goggles and he was flying partially blind.

Desperate to land, Collishaw put down at an aerodrome, expecting help. As he rolled to a stop, he realized that the planes on the tarmac were German Fokkers. He had landed at a German aerodrome. Gunning the engine, he took off with two Fokkers in hot pursuit. The Germans managed to hit Collishaw's plane with machine-gun fire, but he escaped and headed for Allied lines.

He finally found a French aerodrome near Verdun and landed safely.

February 1917 saw Collishaw serving with No. 3 Naval Squadron, operating in tandem with the army near Cambrai, France. By April he was with No. 10 Naval Squadron doing coastal patrols. In May 1917, Collishaw was named as the flight commander in charge of B Flight. B Flight was unique for two reasons: almost every man serving was a Canadian; and, despite the disapproval of the British officers he served with, Collishaw had all of the flight's Sopwith Triplanes' cowlings painted black. Soon they were known as the "Black Flight":

> The aircraft of the All-Black Flight were christened with suitably ominous names. Ellis Reid, of Toronto, flew *Black Roger*; J.E. Sharman, of Winnipeg, flew *Black Death*; Gerry Nash, of Hamilton, called his machine *Black Sheep*; and Marcus Alexander, of Toronto, christened his

plane the *Black Prince*. The flight commander, Collishaw, flew a machine known simply as the *Black Maria*.[9]

By June 1, 1917, the Black Flight, led by Collishaw, was in the air destroying as many enemy aircraft as they could find. By late June the Black Flight was causing so much havoc that the German High Command gave a direct order that the *Jasta* 11 unit was to do anything it took to destroy the Black Flight.

On June 26, German ace Lieutenant Karl Allmenröder, at the head of the Flying Circus, spotted the Black Flight and attacked, shooting down Gerald Nash. Nash survived and was captured but Collishaw had no way of knowing it. The Canadian ace vowed he would exact revenge on the red airplane with the green tail. The next day Collishaw spotted the plane and raked it with machine-gun fire, killing Allmenröder instantly.

Even von Richthofen, the Red Baron, was not immune to the attacks of the Black Flight. On July 2, 1917, the Baron was wounded and shot down by a British F.E.2d escorted by Collishaw and his elite pilots. The Baron was out of the fight for a month, while Collishaw himself shot down six Albatros scouts in the dogfight.

By July 28, the Sopwith Triplanes of the Black Flight were replaced with Sopwith Camels.

The Black Flight had destroyed eighty-seven enemy aircraft; Collishaw was credited with 27 of those. They had been successful, but it had come at a price. In addition to Nash being a German prisoner, both Sharman and Reid had been killed by anti-aircraft fire.

By January 1918, back on the Western Front after a two-month trip to Canada, Collishaw was in command of No. 3 Naval Squadron and flying the deadly Sopwith Camel to great effect. When the RNAS and the RFC merged on April 1,

Raymond Collishaw at the Red Baron's Funeral. Raymond Collishaw attends the funeral of Baron Manfred von Richthofen, the infamous Red Baron. The First World War was still a war of gentleman, and it was not unusual for those who were once enemies to honour the fallen. Pilots believed they were an elite, no matter which side of the war they were on. Author's Collection.

1918, No. 3 Naval Squadron became No. 203 Squadron Royal Air Force. Collishaw, a newly minted major, remained in command of the new squadron, but was doing less and less flying and more and more paperwork. Nonetheless, Raymond Collishaw finished out the war as the highest scoring RNAS ace and the second-highest scoring Canadian ace, with sixty victories against aircraft and eight destroyed enemy balloons.

James Thomas Byford McCudden

Country: England
Born: March 28, 1895
Died: July 9, 1918
Number of Victories: 57

James McCudden, taking advantage of a little-known rule in the British Army, was allowed to enlist in the Royal Engineers in 1910 at the age of fourteen — as a boy bugler. When he completed his basic training, he was sent to Gibraltar and served there for three years before being drafted into the No. 6 Field Company in Dorset, England.

With his movie-star good looks, "Mac," as the teenager had come to be known, was a hit with the ladies. The fact that he wanted to be a pilot just added to his charms.

In 1913 Mac was finally granted a transfer to the RFC, something he had requested after going for a test flight with his brother Willie. However, the army, in its wisdom, did not make McCudden a pilot, but rather an Air Mechanic 2nd Class. Flying would have to wait.

When the war broke out, Mac, by then an Air Mechanic 1st Class, was immediately sent to

James McCudden. A very young James Mc-Cudden stares at the camera in this official press photograph. McCudden eventually shot down fifty-seven enemy aircraft.
Author's Collection.

France. Over the next few months, the commanding officer of No. 3 Squadron allowed the eager McCudden to occasionally fly along as an observer. Despite being a Flight Sergeant and responsible for all the engines in the squadron, at the tender age of twenty McCudden made up his mind — he needed to be a pilot.

On May 12, 1915, just as Mac was given permission to fly as an air gunner, he received word that his brother William had been killed. William had been a flight instructor with No. 61 Squadron and his death profoundly affected Mac. Still, Mac would not give up on his dream of flying. He progressed from gunner to navigator, and was recommended for pilot training in December 1915. He entered flight school in England in January 1916.

By May 1916, Mac was the proud holder of Flying Certificate 107 as Britain's newest pilot. In June he was named a flight instructor. A month later, McCudden was flying an F.E.2 with No. 20 Squadron out of Clairmarais, France. July 1916 saw him move on to No. 29 Squadron and its DH.2 Scouts.

On September 6, 1916, McCudden had his first victory in the air. Chasing a German two-seater aircraft, McCudden found himself dropping behind the faster enemy plane. In an act of desperation he fired three drums of ammunition from his Lewis machine guns. Three days later the enemy aircraft was found crashed behind German lines.

As he continued to chase the enemy, McCudden became one of the first professional airmen. His background as a mechanic meant that nothing got by his critical eye. His men came to know that guns, aircraft, and tactics were all open to discussion — and improvement.

Alternating between flying in England and in France and Belgium, and while performing

McCudden Portrait, 1918. McCudden died in an aircraft crash when his plane stalled on takeoff. Two of McCudden's brothers would also die flying during the First World War. A fourth brother died later of illness after serving in the RAF.
Author's Collection.

his duties as a flight instructor, Mac continued to pile up the victories during the early part of 1917.

Mac returned to Belgium, to stay, on August 16, 1917. Posted to No. 56 Squadron he scored most of his victories flying the S.E.5a, including nine kills during a six-day period in December 1917.

McCudden won more medals for gallantry (including the Victoria Cross) than any other British airman. In his relatively short career, he gained fifty-seven victories, making him the seventh-highest-scoring ace (German and Allied) in the war.

McCudden died flying, as had his brothers Willie (1915) and John (1918). On July 9, 1918, having accepted the command of No. 60 Squadron, Mac personally picked up a new S.E.5a and headed across the English Channel for Boffles, France. Landing at RAF station Auxi-le-Chateau, France, and having received directions, the British ace moved his aircraft onto the runway. As the little aircraft lifted into the sky, the engine stalled. McCudden tried to get back to the landing strip. As he turned, the aircraft corkscrewed 70 feet (21 metres) into the ground. McCudden suffered a cracked skull and died two hours later at No. 21 Casualty Clearing Station. He was twenty-three.

Andrew Beauchamp-Proctor

Country: South Africa
Born: September 4, 1894
Died: June 21, 1921
Number of Victories: 54

With fifty-four victories in the air, Andrew Beauchamp-Proctor was the most successful of the South African air aces.

Proctor was studying engineering when the war broke out in 1914. Like many other young men enrolled in university, he requested a leave from his studies so he could join the army. Soon he was serving with the Duke of Edinburgh's Own Rifles as a signalman in the German South West Africa campaign.

In August 1915, Proctor was honourably discharged and returned to university while working for the South African Field Telegraph. By March 1917, Proctor knew he had to return to the fighting and he joined the RFC.

Like McCudden, Proctor did not head directly to flight school. He first trained as an Air Mechanic 3rd Class. Once he had received his certifications, he was transferred to the School of Military Aeronautics at Oxford, England.

At only 5 feet 2 inches (157 centimetres) tall, the diminutive Proctor had each plane he was flying modified so he could reach the controls. The seat was raised so he could see over the cockpit, and blocks were added to the rudder bar so he could reach it.

Proctor soloed for the first time on June 10, 1917, after only five hours of practice time. It was not an auspicious start. He crashed his plane on landing, destroying the undercarriage. He was first assigned to No. 84 Bomber Squadron and quickly doubled his flying time to ten hours. Bombers did not inspire Proctor, but everything changed when No. 84 was converted to fighters.

On September 23, 1917, Proctor was over France, under the command of Major William Douglas, who developed his unit into one of the most effective scout squadrons in the war. Together the 84th shot down 323 enemy aircraft and created twenty-five aces.

Proctor became the best of the best, shooting down three times as many of the enemy than anyone else in the squadron, with his first victory recorded on January 3, 1918, over a German two-seater.

By the time he was forced to leave the battlefield, Proctor had tallied sixteen aircraft destroyed, sixteen aircraft out of control, and sixteen balloons destroyed (the most balloons destroyed of any airman in the British Empire).

His success was not based on his flying skill but on deadly accuracy with his machine-guns. Proctor was forced out of the war with a shattered arm when he was hit by ground fire on October 8, 1918.

Proctor died on June 21, 1921, when the Sopwith Snipe he was flying during practice for an airshow spun out and crashed.

Andrew Beauchamp-Proctor Portrait. After shooting down fifty-four aircraft, South African ace Andrew Beauchamp-Proctor would survive the war, only to die in a training accident in June 1921 when his plane crashed during preparation for an airshow in England.
Author's Collection.

Donald MacLaren

Country: Canada
Born: May 28, 1893
Died: July 4, 1988
Number of Victories: 54

For little Donald MacLaren, his time spent living in Calgary was idyllic. The six-year-old had the Alberta prairie as his backyard, and by age eight he was using his own shotgun to hunt prairie chickens and ducks for the family larder.

When Don was eighteen, his family moved to Vancouver, where Don finished high school before enrolling in the Electrical Engineering program at McGill University in Montreal. Things went well until 1914 when Don, wracked with pneumonia, was forced to drop out of school and return to Vancouver.

Don, his father, and his brother Roy moved to Keg River Prairie in northern Alberta (the nearest railway station was 200 miles [322 kilometres] to the south at Peace River Crossing) and opened a fur-trading post. Don thrived in the harsh northern conditions. He drove dog teams, trapped and hunted with the Aboriginal people of the area, and even learned to speak Cree fluently.

While Don was away from the trapping post on business. his brother Roy headed south to

Second Lieutenant D.R. MacLaren. Donald MacLaren, a Canadian, tied Beauchamp-Proctor in shooting down fifty-four of the enemy. McLaren survived the war and lived to age of ninety-six after founding Pacific Airways. Author's Collection.

enlist in the Canadian Army. Don and his father, after a short discussion, decided that they, too, needed to enlist. Selling everything they could. the two men headed to Vancouver. Don chose the RFC and his father, considered too old to serve, was assigned to the Imperial Munitions Board.

Don, serving with "Y" Squadron just outside of Toronto, was first sent to No. 90 Central Training School at Armour Heights and then Camp Borden, both in Ontario. On August 19, 1917, MacLaren received his pilot's licence and was sent to No. 43 Training School at Ternhill, England, to fly the Avro 504. His last stop was training on the Bristol Scout and Sopwith Camel aircraft at No. 34 Training School.

After months of specialized training, Don was sent to France to join the No. 2 Air Stores Depot. The depot provided pilots to any squadron that found themselves short. On November 23, 1917, MacLaren was assigned to No. 46 Squadron.

His first victory came on March 6, 1918. The new pilot, in a Sopwith Camel, was flying with four other aircraft when they spotted three unidentified aircraft. Flying into the sun, the Allied pilots weren't sure if the planes were friend or foe, so they quickly climbed above the planes and recognized them as German fighters.

MacLaren described what happened next: "I was flying next to the leader and as he dove at one machine I went for another. They were all silver-gray and had double tail-planes (this was the Hannoveraner C). When they saw us coming they tried to get away by descending in large curves."[10]

MacLaren and the other pilots chased the German planes. As one of the enemy planes tried to manoeuvre under MacLaren, he sent a burst of machine-gun fire, killing the German pilot and sending the plane crashing to the ground, where it caught fire.

For MacLaren, March 21, 1918, was a good day. He first destroyed a large railway gun at Saint-Pol with four 20-pound bombs dropped from his aircraft — the gun was out of action for the rest of the war. Out of bombs, MacLaren headed for home, but saw immediately in front of him a German L.V.G. two-seater. Firing his machine gun, MacLaren put one hundred rounds into the German plane and sent it crashing to the ground.

Separated from the other Allied planes, MacLaren headed for home once again. However, ground fire forced him to climb to a higher altitude, where he almost crashed into a German observation balloon. Not one to miss a target of convenience, Don downed the balloon and forced the German observer to parachute away from the burning craft.

MacLaren's day was not over. Another L.V.G. flew in front of Don. He fired a sustained burst of machine-gun bullets and sent the plane crashing to the ground. Now he could go home.

In September, MacLaren took command of No. 46 Squadron after the squadron commander was killed in action. MacLaren was credited with fifty-four victories in less than nine months of active service. Perhaps his most famous battle was with German ace Mieczysław Garsztka on October 2, 1918.

Garsztka was born in Poland. He was conscripted into the German Army as an infantryman, but moved to the air service as soon as he could. Assigned to *Jasta* 31, he was the only pilot in the unit to become an ace, shooting down five Allied planes.

As MacLaren engaged Garsztka, the German ace quickly fought back. Soon, Allied pilots James Leith and Cyril Sawyer had joined the fray and were also targeting the German ace. It was too much. Garsztka, wounded and with his plane severely damaged, managed to land his craft behind German lines, where he was hospitalized.

All three Allied fighters shared in the victory.

In late October 1918, MacLaren returned to England with the strangest injury. While wrestling with a group of men from the squadron, MacLaren had broken his leg. MacLaren was in the Royal Flying Corps Hospital when the armistice was signed. He received word that he had been attached to the Royal Canadian Air Force (RCAF) and was in command of the pilots as they transferred to the new air force.

William George "Billy" Barker

Country: Canada
Born: November 3, 1894
Died: March 12, 1930
Number of Victories: 50

Aviation came early to William "Billy" Barker's life. He regularly attended exhibition flights put on by pilots travelling to Dauphin, the small farming town in Manitoba where he was born. Almost from the beginning, he knew that one day he would be a pilot.

Barker was a good student but, with the distractions of horseback riding, shooting, and work on the farm all around him, it was difficult for him to maintain good grades. His marks dipped even more when he joined the 32nd Light Horse, a non-permanent active militia unit based at Roblin, Manitoba.

When the Barker family moved to Winnipeg, and war was declared, Billy decided to join the army rather than continue with his schooling. His choice was the cavalry, and he enlisted with the 1st Canadian

Mounted Rifles (CMR) as a Trooper (Private). In June 1915, his basic training completed, Barker was sent to Shornecliffe Military Camp in England to train as a machine-gunner.

By the time Barker had completed his machine-gun course, it was clear there was little role for cavalry in the mud and trenches of France. Barker's unit, the 1st CMR, were sent to France on September 22, 1915 — without their horses. They had been reduced to simple infantrymen. Barker, horrified by the death and destruction all around him, was soon looking for a way out. The RFC provided the answer.

Barker transferred to No. 9 Squadron of the RFC as a probationary observer in the B.E.2 plane after just six days of training. He was soon in demand, as observers with experience with machine guns were very hard to find. The slow-moving British reconnaissance planes were essay targets for the Fokker E.IIIs, and a good machine-gunner was often the difference between life and death.

By April 1916, Barker was commissioned as a Second Lieutenant assigned to No. 4 Squadron as an observer. His first victory in the air came with No. 15 Squadron on July 21. Barker was flying as an observer in a B.E.2 when they encountered a Roland scout plane. The Roland dove out of the sun, preparing to fire on the seemingly defence-less B.E.2. Barker, sensing the danger, spun in his seat and fired his machine gun at the attacking fighter. The German pilot was hit in the forehead and the plane fell away, crashing into the ground.

Barker officially qualified as an observer on August 27, 1916, and was soon assigned to work with Canadian troops on the ground, assisting with spotting enemy troops and directing artillery. On November 15, Barker and his pilot were flying low over the Ancre River when they saw a large group of German troops preparing to

William Barker in Uniform. William "Billy" Barker, with his fifty air victories, became Canada's and the British Empire's most-decorated airman ever. He received the Victoria Cross, the Distinguished Service Order and Bar, the Military Cross and two Bars, two Italian Silver Medals for Military Valour, and the French Croix de Guerre, and he was mentioned in despatches three times. Author's Collection.

counterattack at Beaumont Hamel. Barker, calling in an emergency "zone call," directed the Allied artillery fire onto the German infantry. His efforts saw 4,000 troops killed, wounded, or scattered, unable to counterattack against the Allies. The First Battle of the Somme was over.

In January 1917, Barker began pilot training, and it was discovered he was a natural-born flyer. With his training completed on February 24, 1917, he was flying B.E.2s and R.E.8s with No. 15 Squadron, assisting with corps co-operation. After again successfully directing artillery to break up a German attack during the Arras Offensive (of which the attack at Vimy Ridge was a part), Barker was assigned to No. 4 Squadron and then, on July 7, transferred to No. 15 Squadron.

Barker was wounded in the head by shrapnel from anti-aircraft fire in August 1917. He passed out in the cockpit, to wake up minutes later to find alcohol being liberally poured down his throat by his observer. Barker just barely managed to land the badly damaged plane.

He was sent back to England and spent a short time as flight instructor there — all the while sending multiple requests to be transferred back to combat flying. The government relented when he buzzed (flew very low over) the flying school's headquarters, and he was sent to C Flight of No. 28 Squadron on the Western Front. Barker was back in combat, this time with the Sopwith Camel he had learned to love as a flight instructor.

William Barker in Shorts. William Barker stands by his aircraft, nattily attired in his uniform with shorts.
Author's Collection.

During his first combat mission back on the Western Front on October 20, 1917, Barker was flying air cover for a bombing mission on Rumbeke Aerodrome. A flight of Albatros D.IIIs flew up to challenge the Allied planes; Barker and the others quickly engaged the enemy and the result was a fifteen-minute dogfight. In the end, Barker got his first kill, shooting the wings off a green Albatros.

Within days Barker reached ace status, shooting down another four enemy airplanes. Two days later he shot his sixth plane — a German fighter.

Barker's career on the Western Front was cut short when his squadron was sent to the Italian front to help counter the Austro-Hungarian offensive at Caporetto. In total, four British and four French squadrons joined the fight.

The Sopwith Camels of Barker's squadron flew almost every day, always with at least four 20-pound Cooper bombs attached. The squadron's orders were simple — hit anything and everything they could. Trains, ammo dumps, fuel supplies, troop formations, and bridges were all fair game. Barker used his time in Italy well, downing many planes and observation balloons.

During the 1917 Christmas holidays, when an unofficial truce was in effect, Barker and two other pilots decided to send the Austrians a Christmas message. They hand-painted a sign that read "*To the Austrian Flying Corps from the English RFC, wishing you a Merry X-Mas*" and jumped into their planes to fly over the Motta Aerodrome and drop their message. They then proceeded to strafe the field, killing twelve Austrians and destroying an unknown number of aircraft. Neither the enemy nor their own commander were happy with the unauthorized flight.

William Barker in German Plane. A photo postcard of William Barker. The original caption reads "Col. Barker VC, in one of the captured German aeroplanes against which he fought his last air battle."

Postcard, Britain's Mastery of the Air.
This photo postcard celebrated the air victories of the allies in France and Belgium. They were popular not just with those in the service but with civilians as well.
Author's Collection.

Barker's Sopwith Camel was the most successful single aircraft in the war. He shot down forty-six aircraft and balloons in the year between September 1917 and September 1918, flying a total of 404 operational hours. When the Camel was broken up, Barker salvaged the clock as a memento but was forced to return it the next day, as "scavenging" was strictly forbidden.

On October 27, 1918, Barker was almost killed in the action that won him the Victoria Cross. While engaging and destroying a German airplane, Barker did not see a Fokker DV II closing in behind him. The German pilot fired shots that shattered the femur in Barker's right leg. Barker spun his plane around and fired back on the Fokker, setting it alight.

During the fight with the DV II, Barker lost a great deal of altitude and found himself in the middle of a flight of more than sixty German planes. The Fokkers all started attacking the Canadian, wounding him in the left leg and left elbow. He finally crashed, but was rescued by soldiers from a Highland Regiment.

Barker was rushed to No. 8 General Hospital in Rouen, France, and lay unconscious for several days. In January 1919, when he had recovered enough to travel, he was sent to England to finish his healing. On his release from hospital he returned to Canada.

Barker was the most decorated combatant in the First World War, in both Canada and the British Empire. He remains today the most decorated Canadian ever. His list of medals include the Victoria Cross, the Distinguished Service Order and Bar, the Military Cross and two Bars, two Italian Silver Medals for Military Valour, and the French Croix de Guerre.

Robert A. Little

Country: Australia
Born: July 19, 1895
Died: May 27, 1918
Number of Victories: 47

Robert Alexander Little, known to everyone as "Alec," had always wanted to fly. He first saw an airplane when Harry Houdini, the famed American escapologist and the first man to fly in Australia, took to the air near Melbourne.

Alec, the son of a Scottish-Canadian father and an Australian mother, was educated at Scotch College in Melbourne. He was an accomplished athlete, medalling in swimming, but a poor student. Alec dropped out of school when he was only fifteen to join his father in selling medical textbooks. When Australia declared war in August 1914, Alec's life changed forever.

Alec applied for pilot training at the Australian Army's Central Flying School in Point Cook. However, he and hundreds of others were rejected when the only four spots available for pilot training were quickly filled. Advised that the only way to be accepted into

the air force was to have completed flight training, the teenager sailed to London in July of 1915. Upon arrival in London, Alec quickly registered for flying lessons at the Royal Aero Club at Hendon — lessons that cost hundreds of pounds (a small fortune at the time). New pilot's licence in hand, Alec applied to the RNAS in October 1915, and was accepted as a probationary flight sub-lieutenant on January 14, 1916.

Sub-Lieutenant Little did not make a great first impression. Alec was told that if he did not shape up he would lose his commission.

Robert A. Little.

Things got better from there on, as Alec settled down and focused on being a good flying officer.

Alec's first assignment in France came in June 1916, and saw him flying bombing raids in the Sopwith 1½ Strutter for the No. 1 Naval Wing out of Dunkirk. In October he moved to No. 8 Squadron RNAS and was on the Western Front flying the Sopwith Pup.

On November 23, 1916, flying northeast of La Bassée, France, Alec scored his first victory, shooting down a German two-seater aircraft. By February he had four more victories and the Distinguished Service Cross for "conspicuous bravery in successfully attacking and bringing down hostile machines."[11]

When his squadron converted to the Sopwith Triplane, Alec began to score victory after victory, racking up twenty-eight victories by July 10, 1917. Most of these were made in a triplane that sported his son's name *Blymp* painted under the cockpit.

Like many aces of the First World War, Alec was not known as a particularly good pilot. After the war Reggie Soar, who served with Alec in No. 8 Squadron, said, "Although not a polished pilot, he was one of the most aggressive ... an outstanding shot with both revolver and rifle"[12] Fellow ace Robert Comptson described Alec as, "not so much a leader as a brilliant lone hand.... Small in stature, with face set grimly, he seemed the epitome of deadliness."[13]

After the war a former commanding officer wrote of Alec: "Little was just an average sort of pilot, with tremendous bravery. Air fighting seemed to him to be just a gloriously exhilarating sport.... he never ceased to look for trouble, and in combat his dashing methods, close range fire and deadly aim made him a formidable opponent, and he was the most chivalrous of warriors. As a man, he was a most lovable character."[14]

Nicknamed "Rikki" after Rudyard Kipling's character Rikki-Tikki-Tavi, a mongoose that was faster than the cobras it hunted, Alec also had a gentler side. Ace Raymond Collishaw called Little "an outstanding character, bold, aggressive and courageous, yet he was gentle and kindly. A resolute and brave man."[15]

A rumour started after the war that Alec had painted his Sopwith Triplane in the colours of his old school, Scotch College. While no proof exists of the paint job, he did once fly with the school colours streaming from his wings. Adding to the legend was his reputation of once landing behind enemy lines to clear a jammed machine gun and then taking off again to rejoin the fight.

In May 27, 1918, Alec responded to reports that German Gotha bombers were spotted near his aerodrome, Ezil le Hamel. Flying solo and by moonlight, he soon found the bombers and closed in for the kill. Suddenly a spotlight on one of the bombers highlighted Alec's aircraft. A bullet sliced through both of his legs. Crash-landing in a field near Noeux, Alec fractured both his ankle and skull. Pinned in his aircraft, he bled to death before he could be rescued. He was only twenty-two years old.

George McElroy

Country: Ireland
Born: May 14, 1893
Died: July 31, 1918
Victories: 47

As a proud Irishman, George McElroy quickly volunteered to serve in the Royal Irish Regiment when war broke out in August of 1914. He was trained as a motorcycle courier and received his commission as a lieutenant in May of 1915 while serving in France.

When the Easter Uprising (a revolt against British rule) of April 1916 broke out in Ireland, George was at home recovering from the effects of having been gassed. All serving soldiers, even those who were injured, were pressed into service to put down the riots. George refused to fire on fellow Irishmen. His punishment for refusing an official order was to be "exiled" to a garrison in the south, far from his home and family.

Recognizing that his army career, for all practical purposes, was at an end, McElroy cast about for a way to get back into the war in France. He seized upon flying and received a trans-

George McElroy.

George McElroy.

fer to the RFC late in 1916. After training at Upavon in February 1917, McElroy was assigned to No. 40 Squadron and flew the Nieuport 17 under the tutelage of ace Mick Mannock.

The Nieuport proved unlucky for McElroy, and it was not until December 28, after changing to the S.E.5, that the first German plane fell to his guns.

McElroy proved to be extremely aggressive and absolutely fearless in the air. By February 18, 1918, he had eleven victories. He took command of a flight in No. 24 Squadron RAF and by March 26 had increased his total to eighteen kills in the air. When he crash-landed after brushing the tops of some trees on April 7, his record was twenty-seven. Only his injuries from that accident seemed to slow him down.

Healed, McElroy returned to the air, and by June he had thirty victories, including two observation balloons. July saw seventeen new victories. Facing new injuries from a rough landing after engaging a German two-seater, on July 20 McElroy was admonished by Mannock for the dangerous maneouvre of following a German plane too low. Ironically, on July 26, Mannock was killed by ground fire.

Five days later, death found McElroy. On July 31, 1918, he destroyed a Hannover C, victory number 47. After reporting the kill he returned to the fight — never to return. Later, as was often the custom, a lone German airplane appeared over McElroy's aerodrome and dropped a message — the ace had been killed by ground fire.

Roderic Dallas

Country: Australia
Born: July 30, 1891
Died: June 1, 1918
Number of Victories: 45

In 1912, American aviator Arthur Burr Stone was in Australia to make the first-ever powered flight in Queensland. Roderic Dallas, living in Mount Morgan, was inspired. He had always been interested in flight, corresponding with other enthusiasts and building his own gliders based on the designs of the Wright brothers and Bell.

However, Roderic, a farm boy, knew he needed money if he was going to pursue his dream. So he and his brother took jobs as miners at the quarries of the Mount Morgan Gold Mine.

Roderic, in his youth, had attended Mount Morgan Boys' School, where he excelled in gymnastics, rugby, and, unexpectedly, amateur theatricals. Like many other boys in Mount Morgan, he joined the local cadet corps, where Roderic quickly rose to the rank of sergeant. When he was old enough, he enlisted in the Mount Morgan Company of the 3rd (Port Curtis) Infantry Battalion and was commissioned as a lieutenant.

Always a big child, and now 6 foot 2 inches (188 centimetres) tall and 220 pounds (101 kilograms), Roderic cut an impressive figure in his uniform. Focused on his military career, he never drank nor swore, and smoked only occasionally. Nothing was going to get in the way of Roderic's goal of flying.

The Australian Flying Corps (AFC) was small and had no available positions when Dallas applied for service in 1914. Like fellow Australian Robert Little, Roderic was advised that the best way to become a military pilot was to apply once he had a pilot's licence.

In 1915 Roderic, the proceeds of his mining work in hand, bought a steamship ticket to England. He was not alone. So many young men were trying to join the ranks of the RFC that there were no training slots, private or military, available. Downhearted, Roderic considered giving up and going to the United States to pursue an acting career.

But he made one more attempt. He spoke with Australian aviator Sidney Pickles and enlisted the help of Australia House (the Australian embassy in London). Miraculously, a pilot's slot was found at the RNAS and Roderic was in. He finished first out of a class of eighty-four and received his pilot's licence on August 5, 1915.

In an era of tiny aircraft and even tinier cockpits, Roderic faced a unique problem. For the duration of his service he had a great deal of trouble getting his giant frame into and out of the planes he flew.

Shortly after joining the No. 1 Naval Wing in Dunkirk, France, on December 3, 1915, as a Flight Sub-Lieutenant, Dallas earned his nickname "Breguet." A fellow officer called the airfield and, impersonating the commanding officer, ordered Dallas to take off immediately in a Breguet aircraft warming up on the tarmac. When Dallas tried to take off, he quickly realized that someone had removed the propeller — from that practical joke, he was known as Breguet.

Dallas got his first victory on April 23, 1916, when he shot down a German Aviatik C. Heavily damaged by anti-aircraft fire, Dallas nonetheless returned to the fray and shot down three more enemy aircraft, winning the Distinguished Service Cross for his actions.

If one airplane was associated with Dallas, it was the Sopwith Triplane. On June 23, 1916, he accepted the first of a number of triplanes he would fly. The victories continued to pile up. In one dogfight, Roderic and a fellow pilot attacked a flight of fourteen enemy planes. For forty-five minutes, at altitudes as high as 18,000 feet (5,500 metres), the two pilots wove and dodged among the German craft, firing all the time. So dogged was their attack that the two British aviators managed to break up the German formation, destroying three planes and forcing the balance into retreat.

By March 1918, Roderic was the Major Commanding of No. 40 Squadron. He was well respected by his men and took his role of mentor and instructor seriously. As his personal tally of enemy aircraft climbed to thirty-nine, he spent hours coaching his men on how to avoid traps set by enemy pilots and how to be aggressive without being careless. Out of affection, his men changed his nickname from Breguet to Admiral, to reflect his experience with the RNAS.

By June 1, 1918, Roderic had forty-five victories to his credit and had risen to the rank of Lieutenant-Colonel. However, Dallas did not live to enjoy his new rank. On the day of his promotion, he headed out on a solo mission over Lievin, France. He encountered three Fokker triplanes from German unit *Jasta* 14. As Dallas engaged one aircraft, another, piloted by Jasta commanding officer *Leutnant* Johannes Werner and supported by two others, gained the advantage and shot down Dallas from above. Dallas's body was later recovered from no man's land.

FIVE

The Enemy Aces

Top Ten German Aces

Manfred von Richthofen — 80 victories

Ernst Udet — 62 victories

Erich Löwenhardt — 54 victories

Werner Voss — 48 victories

Josef Jacobs — 48 victories

Fitz Rumey — 45 victories

Rudolph Berthold — 44 victories

Bruno Larzen — 44 victories

Paul Bauner — 43 victories

Oswald Boelcke — 40 victories

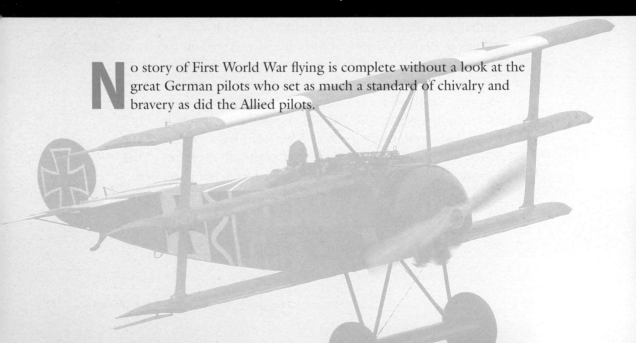

No story of First World War flying is complete without a look at the great German pilots who set as much a standard of chivalry and bravery as did the Allied pilots.

Manfred Albrecht Freiherr von Richthofen

Country: Germany
Born: May 2, 1892
Died: April 21, 1918
Number of Victories: 80

If there is one name that everyone knows from the First World War, it is Baron Manfred von Richthofen, the Red Baron.

In 1911, at the age of nineteen, Manfred von Richthofen, like many future pilots on the both the German and Allied sides, joined a cavalry unit — the *Ulanen-Regiment Kaiser Alexander der III. von Russland (1. Westpreußisches) Nr. 1*—1st Emperor Alexander III of Russia Uhlan Regiment (1st West Prussia Regiment) — assigned to the *3. Eskadron* (No. 3 Squadron) based in Milicz, Poland.

By the time the war broke out in 1914, Richthofen had been promoted to officer of a reconnaissance unit, and was soon seeing action in Russia, France, and Belgium. Again, like many cavalry officers on the Allied side, Richthofen saw the romance quickly evaporate from the mounted service. With trench warfare, the horse was more of a liability than an asset, and Richthofen's unit was soon dismounted and turned into dispatch runners and field telephone operators. When the future ace was ordered to the supply branch, he knew his time was up.

In 1915 Richthofen requested a transfer to the Imperial German Army Air Service — the *Luftstreitkräfte*. He supposedly wrote on his request, "I have not gone to war in order to collect cheese and eggs, but for another purpose."[16] In May 1915 his request to fly was granted.

Manfred von Richthofen was born on May 2, 1892, in Breslau, Germany (now Wrocław, Poland). As the son of a minor Imperial German nobleman, he was entitled to use the title of *Freiherr* or Baron. Manfred, which means "Man of Peace," was named after a great-uncle who had risen high in the ranks in the Prussian Army.

The young Richthofen was athletic, riding horses and hunting almost daily on his father's estate. In the gym he competed in gymnastics and frequently won awards for his prowess. Manfred, like many sons of minor noble families, was educated by tutors at home before transferring to a formal school at Schweidnitz, Germany. When he turned eleven, he joined a local cadet corps.

The future ace fell in love with flying the first time he had the chance to get airborne. Richthofen described his first experience with flight in his 1917 autobiography:

> I had been told the name of the place to which we were to fly and I was to direct the pilot. At first we flew straight ahead, then the pilot turned to the right, then left. I had lost all sense of direction over our own aerodrome…! I didn't care a bit where I was, and when the pilot thought it was time to go down, I was disappointed. Already I was counting down the hours to the time we could start again.[17]

During the summer of 1915, Richthofen was an observer with *Flieger-Abteilung* (Flying Squadron) 69, flying reconnaissance missions on the Eastern Front. When the squadron was transferred to the Champagne region of France, Richthofen got his first air victory by shooting down a French Farman aircraft, but the kill could not be verified so he received no credit.

October 1915 saw Richthofen training as a pilot, and in March 1916 he was assigned to a bomber squadron *Kampfgeschwader* 2, flying the Albatros C.III. It was not a promising start. During his first flight in the Albatros he crash-landed.

However, learning from his mistake, Richthofen quickly distinguished himself as a fighter pilot when he transferred to *Jasta* 2 in 1916, winning his first credited aerial combat over Cambrai, France, on September 17, 1916. He had engaged a British pilot and, as the two men fought to gain the advantage, the planes came close enough to each other to risk a mid-air collision.

Red Baron Uniform, Close-Up. Perhaps the most famous of the First World War aces was Manfred von Richthofen, the Red Baron. He would be credited with eighty victories; i.e., eighty Allied aircraft shot down before he, himself, was shot down. At his neck he wears the Pour le Mérite medal, Prussia's highest military award.
Author's Collection.

Ultimately, Richthofen shot off the British plane's propeller, disabling the plane. The pilot managed to land, but died later in hospital of his wounds.

With his first victory completed, Richthofen started a personal tradition of ordering a silver cup engraved with the date and type of enemy aircraft for each plane he shot down. By the time his collection had grown to sixty cups, silver had become a rationed metal. The German government ordered that all silver be reserved for war production only. Not wanting to use pewter cups, because he felt they did not honour his enemies, Richthofen suspended his collection — but not the victories.

Richthofen was not known as a spectacular pilot, but rather as a brilliant tactician. His brother Lothar had forty kills, each one showing a daring use of his aircraft and sheer luck. For Manfred the flying gospel was a set of maxims known as *Dicta Boeleke* that dictated every moment of air combat, all designed to ensure victory. While von Richthofen respected his brother's success, he believed that combat flying was a science, not an art, and that tactics were more important than acrobatics. He was determined that luck would play no part in his victories.

Like the British ace Mick Mannock, whose principles of air combat were similar to his own, von Richthofen believed that it was possible to plan a dogfight from beginning to end. Like all great aces. Richthofen became a student of air combat and insisted on knowing everything he could about both his own plane and the planes of his enemies.

Richthofen was quoted as saying: "I never get into an aircraft for fun. I aim first for the head of the pilot, or rather at the head of the observer, if there is one."[18]

Over the next year Richthofen continued to rack up victories, flying a variety of aircraft. January 1917 was a spectacularly successful month for the German ace. He was promoted to command of *Jasta* 11 and, after his sixteenth kill, was awarded the Pour le Mérite, or the Blue Max, the highest award in Germany at the time.

In January 1917, for the first time, Richthofen painted his airplane bright red. With the signature colour, combined with his title of Baron, he quickly became known to Allied pilots and the public as The Red Baron (a name the British media quickly picked up). However, in German he was referred to as *Der Rote Kampfflieger*, translated as The Red Battle Flyer or The Red Fighter Pilot.

In April 1917, the Bloody April when Allied pilots seemed unable to gain victories against the German aces, Richthofen shot down twenty-two British aircraft, four in one day.

June 1917 saw Richthofen again rewarded with a promotion, this time to the command of the new, larger *Jagdgeschwader* 1 (*Jastas* 4, 6, 10, and 11) — the infamous Flying Circus. Richthofen built the *Jagdgeschwad*er around the ideal of mobility. His unit was able to move at a moment's notice to where it was needed. It revolutionized the idea of air combat. Richthofen and his pilots focused on tactics rather than acrobatics. He instructed every pilot in his command that they were to "Aim for the man and don't miss him. If you are fighting a two-seater, get the observer first; until you have silenced the gun, don't bother about the pilot."[19]

By this time, the Red Baron was a national hero in Germany and was both feared and respected by the Allies. While chasing an enemy two-seater reconnaissance plane on July 7, 1917, he was struck in the head by a bullet fired by the observer in the enemy plane, leaving a deep, two-inch long wound. While the wound proved nearly fatal, Richthofen managed to land his plane and was sent home to Germany to recover. He later said the wound was his own fault, as he had misjudged the distance to the enemy plane and thought he was safely out of range.

Richthofen's fame was now nearly complete and, as he recovered in Germany, he was greeted by adoring fans everywhere he went and feted by the rich and famous. The Red Baron became such a symbol of valour and national pride that the German High Command wanted to ground him, fearing his death would devastate German morale. Richthofen refused the safe route and returned to air combat on August 6, 1917.

Red Baron in Aircraft. While the Red Baron is most often pictured in a triplane — a plane with three stacks of wings — he flew many aircraft during his military career. Richthofen is pictured here sitting in the cockpit of a German fighter aircraft.
Author's Collection.

The High Command had good reason to worry about their national hero. Despite his protestations that he was fully recovered, Richthofen suffered constant headaches and bouts of weakness. It would prove to be a mistake to return to the battlefield so soon.

At 11:00 a.m. on April 21, 1918, Richthofen was flying from the German aerodrome at Cappy, France. He was chasing a Sopwith Camel flown by Canadian Lieutenant Wilfred "Wop" May of No. 209 Squadron RAF low over Allied lines. Fellow Canadian pilot Captain Arthur "Roy" Brown saw that May was in trouble and attacked Richtofen from above and to the left of his aircraft. The German ace was hit in the chest by a single .303 bullet. Severely wounded, Richthofen managed to land his aircraft behind Australian lines, but soldiers who closed in on the aircraft said he died shortly after they arrived.

While Brown received the credit for the death of the Red Baron, historians later discovered that a bullet from the ground, not from an aircraft, shot down the great German ace. Brown said little about the controversy.

The Red Baron was buried near Amiens, France, in the 1st Uhlans uniform that he was wearing when he was shot down. The service was conducted by the Australian Flying Corps, and twelve Australian flying officers acted as his pallbearers.

When the final tally was done, Baron Manfred von Richthofen, the Red Baron, had shot down eighty Allied planes. What is remarkable is that seventy-nine of those had been British aircraft, and he had personally accounted for the death, wounding, of capture of 126 British airmen.

Ernst Udet

Country: Germany
Born: April 26, 1896
Died: November 17, 1941
Number of Victories: 62

At first glance, Colonel-General Ernst Udet did not impress anyone as a person who would become one of Germany's greatest aces. Udet was born in 1896 and tried to join the army in August 1914, but was rejected for being too short, at only 5 feet, 3 inches (160 centimetres).

Always optimistic, Udet refused to let the rejection stop him from serving in the military. In 1914 the German army called for volunteers to become motorcycle dispatch riders, but only if the volunteers had their own machines. Udet did (it had been a gift from his father) and was accepted into the 26th Wurttemberg Reserve Division.

Always interested in flying, Udet had established the Munich Aero-Club in 1909, and first met military pilots when he was convalescing after a motorcycle accident. The pilots convinced him to try flying rather than returning to the motorcycle service. It was just the chance Udet was waiting for.

For Germans interested in flying for their country, training spots for observers or pilots were few and far between in the early days of the war. Undeterred, Udet found that if he had a private pilot's licence he would be immediately admitted to the German Army Air Service. Two thousand marks and hours of training later he had a pilot's licence — and a job in the army.

In December 1915, flying the Fokker E.III, at the time the most deadly plane on either side of the conflict, Udet was by himself looking for the enemy over the Vosges sector of the Western Front. Suddenly a French Caudron G.4 appeared on the horizon. As the enemy plane approached, Udet got what is known to hunters as "buck fever" — in the excitement of the movement he forgot all his training. Rather than trying to get above and behind the French plane, Udet flew straight at it.

With the French plane close enough for Udet to make out the facial features of both the enemy pilot and the observer, the German pilot froze. He could not fire his guns. The French observer had no such problem and fired into Udet's plane. Bullets tore into the aircraft and something hit Udet in the face, opening up a long cut. Snapping out of his fear, Udet dove downward into the cover provided by a nearby cloud and lost the pursuing enemy plane. Back at his own base, his wound treated, Udet swore he would never make the same mistakes again.

Udet in Front of Airplane in Hangar. Ernst Udet shot down sixty-two Allied aircraft — his total was second only to the Red Baron in the German military. This record earned him the Pour le Mérite medal as well.
Author's Collection.

Udet earned his first kill during an encounter with twenty-three French planes on March 18, 1916. This time, flying the Fokker D.III, Udet downed a Farman F.40. He later described the encounter: "The fuselage of the Farman dives down past me like a giant torch.... A man, his arms and legs spread out like a frog's, falls past — the observer. At the moment, I don't think of them as human beings. I feel only one thing — victory, triumph, victory."[20]

From then on, his lesson well-learned, Udet took the task of flying seriously. He focused on tactics, and his flying skills became better and better each time he flew.

Recognizing Udet's skills as a pilot, Manfred von Richthofen invited the pilot to join his famed Flying Circus. When von Richthofen saw Udet down an enemy airplane in a frontal attack, Udet was made commanding officer of *Jasta* 11.

When Udet received a new Fokker DR.I triplane, he had the plane painted red to match the Baron's, but Udet's upper wing was painted with alternating red and white stripes. He also had the name *Lo* (after his girlfriend Lola Zonk) painted on the fuselage, and on the tail, the words *Du-doch-nicht* (in English, "Certainly not you"). The taunt was not lost on enemy pilots.

Udet's men considered him a great leader. He spent hours teaching new pilots both tactics and marksmanship. Udet felt that victory in the air came from better training and less bravado.

Going on to be Germany's second highest scoring ace with sixty-two confirmed victories, Udet had another distinction. He was the first pilot to survive bailing out of an aircraft with a parachute. On June 29, 1918, he was in combat with a French Breguet when his plane's controls were shot away and the aircraft

Udet in Flight Suit. Ernst Udet would survive the First World War and go on to help build the Luftwaffe for Second World War Germany. He was a national hero, but by 1941 he was having disagreements with Hermann Goering, the head of the Luftwaffe and another First World War German ace, as well as with the Nazi Party. On November 31, 1941, Udet committed suicide. Author's Collection.

spiralled uncontrollably toward the earth. Udet was forced to bail out, but had on the new Heinecke parachute and landed safely.

On September 28, 1918, Udet received a wound to his thigh that kept him out of the rest of the war. The German ace went on to fly for the German Luftwaffe in the Second World War, but committed suicide when faced with political and personal pressures from within the German Air Force.

Erich Löwenhardt

Country: Germany
Born: April 7, 1897
Died: August 10, 1918
Number of Victories: 54

Germany's third-highest-scoring ace, Erich Löwenhardt, graduated from military school in Lichterfelde in 1914 — just in time for the start of the First World War.

Unlike many of his contemporaries Löwenhardt did not join the cavalry but rather Infantry Regiment No. 141, fighting on the Eastern Front. He was wounded near Lodz, Poland, but stayed with his unit, becoming the standard bearer at the Battle of Tannenberg, August 23–30, 1914. For his bravery Löwenhardt was commissioned as an officer on October 2, 1914.

Less than a month later, on October 30, Löwenhardt was wounded and received the Iron Cross 2nd Class. He was sent back to Germany to recover from his wounds, but was soon back at the front — this time in the Carpathians leading the famed ski troops. Proving his personal bravery once again, Löwenhardt saved the lives of five wounded men and received the Iron Cross 1st Class. After being transferred to the Alpine Corps on the Italian Front, he became too sick to serve and was sent home.

Löwenhardt refused to stay out of the battle. Within five months he had recovered and volunteered for service with the Imperial German Army Air Service. Recognizing both his experience and bravery, the Air Service quickly accepted him as an aerial observer.

Unsatisfied with sitting in the back seat of the airplane, Löwenhardt turned his focus to becoming a pilot, completing pilot school in 1916. He was soon flying two-seater planes with *Flieger-Abteilung (Artillerie)*, or Flyer Detachment (Artillery), 265.

Craving even more combat, Löwenhardt attended fighter-pilot training in January 1917, and in March was assigned to *Jagdstaffel* 10. On March 24 he gained his first aerial victory, shooting down an observation balloon near Récicourt, France.

The courage Löwenhardt had shown as a foot soldier was clearly evident in his focused and deadly flying. Assigned both Albatros and Pfalz airplanes, he was soon an ace, with his fifth victory on September 21.

Löwenhardt narrowly missed death on November 6, 1917, when, as he flew over Winkel Saint Éloi, Belgium, an anti-aircraft shell slammed into the left wingtip of his aircraft. The shell failed to explode, but did tear away a large portion of the wing. The airplane immediately went into a spin, its nose heading straight for the earth. At just 50 feet (15 metres) above the ground, Löwenhardt managed to pull out of the death dive and put the plane down in an emergency landing. The aircraft, making contact with the ground, tumbled end over end before coming to rest. Amazingly, the German ace walked away from the wreck with only minor injuries.

In 1917, Löwenhardt gathered up a total of eight confirmed aerial victories — four balloons and four airplanes. He started 1918 out with two kills, a balloon, and a Bristol F.2 fighter; March saw five more victories. He was a methodical pilot who preferred to use tactics and training rather than bravado and daring in dogfights.

The victories and the medals continued to pile up. On April 1, 1918, Löwenhardt, at just twenty years old, was made the commanding officer of *Jasta* 10 of the Flying Circus. They were flying the new Fokker DV.IIs, his own painted a bright yellow.

He qualified for the Blue Max medal with his twentieth kill on May 10, another observation balloon. By the end of July, Löwenhardt had nine balloons and thirty-nine airplanes to his credit.

August 1918 proved devastating to the German Army — and fatal to Löwenhardt. For

Löwenhardt in Front of Airplane in Leather Jacket. Erich Löwenhardt claimed fifty-four Allied aircraft before he was killed in combat. Author's Collection.

Löwenhardt, the beginning of the Battle of Amiens, France, on August 8, 1918, was a time of "happy hunting." On the first day of the battle he downed three RAF aircraft, and two more on August 9.

The next day, despite a badly sprained ankle, Löwenhardt led a flight of German fighters against No. 56 Squadron RAF. At 12:15 p.m. he quickly shot down a British S.E.5a over Chaulnes, France, which was kill number 54.

The Red Baron's brother Lothar von Richthofen described the battle in an article entitled "My Last Time at the Front":

> Löwenhardt in his bright yellow machine was right behind the Englishman. I saw right away that everyone else was superfluous. But four or five of them didn't realize this, and were flying right behind Löwenhardt. Then, all of a sudden, I see the Englishman dive straight down, a trail of smoke behind him. … But what's that? Löwenhardt is no longer flying behind the downed Englishman — just a chaotic mess of thousands of splinters.[21]

As he and the other German pilots turned for home, Löwenhardt crashed his plane into one flown by *Leutnant* (Lieutenant) Alfred Wenz, who was flying for *Jasta* 11. As the planes plummeted to the ground, Löwenhardt and Wenz, both equipped with parachutes, leaped from their respective aircraft. As he drifted downward, Wenz watched as Löwenhardt crashed into the earth — his parachute failing to open. The German ace was dead.

Josef Jacobs

Country: Germany
Born: May 15, 1894
Died: July 29, 1978
Number of Victories: 48

Josef Carl Peter Jacobs tied with Werner Voss as Germany's fourth-highest-scoring ace. He also had the distinction of surviving the war and living on to fight again.

The young Jacobs was smitten by flying early in his life when, as a boy in Bonn, he watched the planes take off and land at the flying school in Hangelar. After learning to fly at the same school, Jacobs was

Josef Jacobs in Aircraft. Josef Jacobs in his aircraft after the end of the war. Allied troops crowd in to get their photo taken with the famous German ace.
Author's Collection.

quickly accepted as a pilot trainee in the Imperial German Army Air Service's *Fliegerersatz Abteilung* (Replacement Detachment) 9.

July 3, 1915, found Jacobs flying long-range missions over Allied lines with *FA* 11 (Reconnaissance). However, it was not until May 1916 that he scored an aerial victory. Since April, he had been flying a Fokker E.III Eindecker with *Fokkerstaffel-West*. On May 12 he engaged a two-seater Caudron that was flying without an observer. After a short fight, Jacobs sent the enemy plane crashing to the ground. While it was his first kill, it was unconfirmed because there were no independent witnesses to the action.

At the end of the month *Fokkerstaffel-West* was ordered from a combat role so that they could fly air cover over the General Headquarters at Charleville, France. Within a month, Jacobs had applied for a transfer, believing that his time was being wasted playing "babysitter" to the German staff at headquarters. He was granted his request and returned to the front, again flying a Fokker E.III.

On September 19 Jacobs received the improved Fokker DV.II, just in time to fall violently ill with dysentery. Confined to his bed for several weeks, he chafed to get airborne again. When *Fokkerstaffel-West* became *Jasta* 12 on October 6, 1916, Jacobs elected to

Josef Jacobs in Uniform with Man in Suit. Tied with Voss, Josef Jacobs claimed forty-eight victories in the air. After the First World War, Jacobs flew with the Turkish military as a trainer. He would live in Germany as a prosperous businessman until his death in 1978.
Author's Collection.

stay with his unit, but transferred to *Jasta* 22 in November when an opportunity to serve under his old friend *Oberleutnant* Erich Hönemanns came up.

It was a fortuitous change. In January 1917 Jacobs got his second kill — a Canadian Caudron R.4. What quickly followed were three more official kills and eight unconfirmed. Yet, on August 2, 1917, when an opportunity to command *Jasta* 7 came up, Jacobs leaped at the chance.

In January 1918 Jacobs received a new Fokker DR.I triplane, which he flew until the end of the war. Painted in distinctive black livery, Jacobs's plane was soon well-known to all pilots in the air over France. Jacobs would make thirty kills in the triplane, making him the highest-scoring German ace in that particular aircraft.

Jacobs received the coveted Blue Max on July 19, 1918.

After the armistice in November 1918, Jacobs signed up to fight against the Bolsheviks (communists) in the Baltic region. When it was clear the Bolsheviks would win the revolution in Russia, Jacobs became a flight instructor for the Turkish government.

Jacobs, after becoming a noted First World War historian, passed away in Munich on July 29, 1978.

Werner Voss

Country: Germany
Born: April 13, 1897
Died: September 23, 1917
Number of Victories: 48

Described by British ace James McCudden as "the bravest German airman," Werner Voss was being groomed to take over the family dye factory as storm clouds gathered over Germany in early 1914. However, Voss had a different idea. He fully intended to serve his country in the military and, in April 1914, he lied about his age to join *Ersatz Eskadron* 2, attached to the 11th Hussar Regiment. Voss was not drawn to the Hussar Regiment's horses but to motorcycles, and on August 2, 1914, he graduated as a motorcyclist in the German Army.

After war was declared, Voss gave up his motorcycles to work as an army recruiter, convincing young men to join the Hussars. On November 16, 1914, Voss signed up himself, and by November 30 he was on the Eastern Front facing combat for the first time, this time mounted on a horse.

Werner Voss in Cockpit. By the time he was killed in battle at age twenty, Werner Voss had downed forty-eight Allied aircraft.
Author's Collection.

Voss had a mixed record on the Eastern Front. He was promoted twice, received the Iron Cross 2nd Class, and was accepted to the officer training school at Beckstadt. He graduated on July 26, 1915, but was sent to the reserves as unfit for combat based on his flat feet.

Refusing to be sidelined, Voss put in for a transfer to the Imperial German Army Air Service and was accepted on August 1, 1915, entering *Fliegerersatz-Abteilung* (Training Detachment) 7 in Cologne.

Voss flew his first solo flight on September 28 and graduated on February 12, 1916. The ink was hardly dry on his flight certificate when he applied to become an instructor. On March 2, Voss became the youngest flight instructor in the German Air Service, though he did not receive his own instructor's licence until May 28, 1916.

Next, Voss was posted to *Jasta* 2, flying a single-seat scout aircraft. It was here that he met Manfred von Richthofen, the Red Baron. The two pilots became fast friends, flying as wingmen. Despite the fact that Voss came from a wealthy family and Richthofen from a noble, but less wealthy, family, they often visited each other's homes.

On November 26, 1916, Voss scored his first aerial victory in the morning and his second in the afternoon, a feat that earned him the Iron Cross 1st Class in December. By the end of March 1917, he had another eleven kills, with two of them coming within ten minutes of each other on March 17. On April 8, 1917, Voss received the Blue Max, recognizing his twenty-plus aerial victories.

As his victories continued, Voss became acting commander of *Jasta* 29 on June 28, 1917, and then, five days later, temporary commander of *Jasta* 14. It did not end there. On July 30, Voss became the commander of *Jasta* 10. He was now flying with Richthofen and his Flying Circus.

Voss was a talented mechanic and often tinkered with the planes

Voss and Richthofen. Werner Voss (left) and Manfred von Richthofen (right) flew together in combat. Voss was killed on September 23, 1917, when he faced eight British aces in single combat. Famous British ace James McCudden described Voss as "the bravest German airman."
Author's Collection.

German Aviator Dropping a Bomb. A German aviator drops a bomb somewhere on the Western Front, circa 1918.

in his command, trying to squeeze more speed and performance out of each of them. In August 1917, Voss was personally sent one of only two new Fokker DR.Is in existence. (Baron von Richthofen got the other.) Voss thought the plane was an exceptional fighter and decorated his by painting a face on the cowling. Flying the DR.I, Voss added another fourteen victories to his record.

In September 11, 1917, when Voss took an extended leave to Germany, his record was second only to Richthofen's — forty-seven victories to sixty-one.

On his return from Germany, Voss was flying, on September 23, 1917, when he encountered eight Allied aces over the battlefield at Passchendaele. In one of the greatest dogfights of the First World War, Voss managed to damage each of the Allied planes without suffering any damage to his own. Suddenly, a bullet hit the German ace. His plane continued on a straight, undeviating course, indicating to the pursuing pilots that he was probably injured. British Lieutenant Arthur Rhys-Davids saw his chance and moved in behind Voss's plane. A burst from the British plane's machine guns brought down the DR.I and Voss.

Recalling the action, British ace James McCudden later commented:

> I shall never forget my admiration for that German pilot, who single handed, fought seven of us for ten minutes.... I saw him go into a fairly steep dive and so I continued to watch, and then saw the triplane hit the ground and disappear into a thousand fragments, for it seemed to me that it literally went into powder.[22]

When the crash site was discovered days later, Voss's body was recovered and later buried at the German war cemetery at Langemark.

SIX

The Airplanes

July 14, 1915: The Curtiss JN-3 training biplane is
the first Canadian mass-produced airplane.

Some of the airplanes of the First World War — like the Sopwith
Camel and the Fokker DR.I triplane — became icons known to
anyone who followed the war in Europe. Others made only brief
appearances in battle, and were quickly overtaken by advancing technology.

For the pilots, their airplanes were the difference between life and death.
Aircraft were judged by their speed, maneuvrability, and reliability. Planes
that could not keep up with the enemy were quickly abandoned; those
that could outperform the enemy became personal favourites of the pilots.

In the end, surviving air combat required the best pilots flying the
best planes.

Allied Airplanes*

Sopwith Camel

For Allied pilots in the First World War, the Sopwith Camel was the
ultimate fighter aircraft. After the Sopwith Pup, the Camel was the

---

* Where specifications are missing, the information was not available.

next generation of fighter. Named for the small hump created by the extension of the trailing edge of the plane's cockpit, the Camel had a powerful engine and well-balanced controls, supported by a high cruising speed and exceptional balance. The plane could "turn on a dime," which made it a formidable fighter and a pilot's favourite. Media of the day describe the Camel as "a small bird of prey."

Flown by: Collishaw, MacLaren, Barker

General Specifications

Manufacturer: Sopwith Aviation Company
Designer: Herbert Smith
First Flight: December 22, 1916
Introduced: June 1917
Retired: January 1920
Primary User: RFC, RNAS, AFC
Number Built: 5,490
Crew: One
Length: 18 feet, 9 inches (5.71 metres)
Wingspan: 28 feet (8.53 metres)
Height: 8 feet, 6 inches (2.59 metres)
Wing Area: 231 square feet (21.46 square metres)
Empty Weight: 930 pounds (420 kilograms)
Loaded Weight: 1,455 pounds (660 kilograms)
Power Plant: 1 × Clerget 9B 9 cylinder rotary engine, 130 horsepower (97 kilowatt)

148th Aero Squadron, "American" Sopwith Camels. While these are American Sopwith Camels of the U.S. 148th American Aero Squadron, the Camel was flown by the Allies after its delivery to the Western Front in 1917. Pilots would complain about the handling of the Sopwith Camel, but the plane recorded 1,294 downed enemy aircraft.
Author's Collection.

Performance

Maximum Speed: 115 mph (185 km/h)
Cruise Speed: 85 mph (137 km/h)
Stall Speed: 48 mph (77 km/h)
Range: 300 miles (485 kilometres)
Endurance: 2.5 hours
Service Ceiling: 21,000 feet (6,400 metres)
Rate of Climb: 1,085 feet per minute (330 metres per minute)

Armament

Guns: 2 × 0.303-inch (7.7-millimetre) Vickers machine guns

Sopwith 1 Strutter

The Sopwith 1½ Strutter was named for the arrangement of the struts supporting the top wing, which were paired one long and one short. The Strutter was the first two-seater fighter on the Allied side, and was armed with fixed Vickers machine guns that were synchronized to fire through the propeller. A formidable fighter, the Strutter was also used as a reconnaissance plane and a bomber.

Flown by: Collishaw, Little

General Specifications

Manufacturer: Sopwith Aviation Company
Designer: Based on Herb Smith design
First Flight: December 1915
Introduced: April 1916
Retired: Used post-war as a trainer
Primary User: RFC, RNAS, Aéronautique Militaire
Number Built: 4,500 by France; 1,439 by Great Britain
Crew: Two (pilot and observer)
Length: 25 feet, 3 inches (7.70 metres)
Wingspan: 33 feet, 6 inches (10.21 metres)
Height: 10 feet, 3 inches (3.12 metres)
Wing Area: 346 square feet (32.16 square metres)
Empty Weight: 1,305 pounds (593 kilograms)
Loaded Weight: 2,149 pounds (975 kilograms)

Power Plant: 1 × Clerget 9B rotary engine, 130 horsepower (97 kilowatt)

Performance

Maximum Speed: 100 mph (161 km/h)
Cruise Speed: 88 mph (142 km/h)
Range: 340 miles (565 kilometres)
Endurance: 3.75 hours
Service Ceiling: 15,500 feet (4,730 metres)
Rate of Climb: 650 feet per minute (198 metres per minute)

Armament

Guns: 1 × .303-inch (7.7-millimetre) forward-firing synchronized Vickers machine gun; 1 × .303-inch (7.7-millimetre) Lewis gun in observer's cockpit
Bombs: Up to 130 pounds (60 kilograms)

Sopwith 1 Strutter, Front. The Sopwith 1 Strutter was flown by both British and French Forces. The plane was unique, as the first Allied aircraft to be equipped with synchronized machine guns that allowed the pilot to fire through the spin of the propeller, making the guns much more accurate. Author's Collection.

Sopwith Triplane

In an effort to create a more manoeuvrable fighter, designer Herbert Smith set out to create a plane with the proven three-wing configuration. The result was the Sopwith Triplane. Like the Sopwith Camel, the Triplane was a small, compact airplane, but the increased wing area gave the plane a superior climb rate. With a high maximum speed and good manoeuvrability, the Sopwith Triplane was often the victor in dogfights and discouraged enemy attacks: Allied pilots reported that German pilots often turned away from a fight when the Sopwith Triplanes made their appearance.

Flown by: Collishaw, Little, Dallas

General Specifications

Manufacturer: Sopwith Aviation Company
Designer: Herbert Smith
First Flight: May 28, 1916
Introduced: December 1916
Retired: 1917
Primary User: RNAS
Number Built: 147

Sopwith Triplane. The Sopwith Triplane, nicknamed the Tripehound or the Tripe, had a successful war record, but was withdrawn when the Sopwith Camel was introduced into the war. The Tripe would finish its career as a trainer for new pilots.

Crew: One
Length: 18 feet, 10 inches (5.73 metres)
Wingspan: 26 feet, 6 inches (8 metres)
Height: 10 feet, 6 inches (3.2 metres)
Wing Area: 231 square feet (21.46 square metres)
Empty Weight: 1,101 pounds (500 kilograms)
Loaded Weight: 1,541 pounds (700 kilograms)
Power Plant: 1 × Clerget 9B rotary engine, 130 horsepower (97 kilowatts)

Performance

Maximum Speed: 117 mph (187 km/h) at 5,000 feet (1,830 metres)
Cruise Speed: 105 mph (170 km/h)
Stall Speed: 44 mph (170 km/h)
Range: 280 miles (450 kilometres)
Endurance: 2 hours, 45 minutes
Service Ceiling: 20,500 feet (6,250 metres)
Rate of Climb: 1000 feet per minute (304 metres per minute)

Armament

Guns: 1 × .303-inch (7.7-millimetre) Vickers machine gun

Curtiss JN-4 (Jenny)

The Curtis JN-4 (nicknamed the "Jenny") was originally built as a trainer, and many First World War pilots learned to first fly at the stick of the Jenny. While not a combat aircraft, the Jenny had a huge influence on the course of aviation after the war. Many surplus Jennys were sold to pilots returning home from Europe, and they quickly became common at barnstorming shows across North America. For many Canadians and Americans, the Jenny was the iconic airplane throughout the 1920s.

Flown by: None of the aces

General Specifications

Manufacturer: Curtiss
Designer: Benjamin D. Thomas
First Flight: 1915
Introduced: 1915

Curtiss Jenny. The Curtiss JN-4 or Jenny (named for the JN designation), this one a modern-day replica, saw service throughout the First World War. When the war ended, the Jenny became a common sight at barnstorming shows across North America, as thousands of the planes were sold to civilians as surplus.

Retired: Used well past end of war for both military and civilian purposes
Primary User: Army Air Service, RFC
Number Built: 6,813
Crew: Two
Length: 27 feet, 4 inches (8.33 metres)
Wingspan: 43 feet, 7¾ inches (13.3 metres)
Height: 9 feet, 10½ inches (3.01 metres)
Wing Area: 352 square feet (32.7 square metres)
Empty Weight: 1,390 pounds (630 kilograms)
Loaded Weight: 1,920 pounds (871 kilograms)
Power Plant: 1 × Curtiss OX-5 V8 piston, 90 horsepower (67 kilowatts)

Performance

Maximum Speed: 75 mph (121 km/h)
Cruise Speed: 60 mph (97 km/h)
Stall Speed: 45 mph (72 km/h)
Range: 155 miles (250 kilometres)
Endurance: 2 hours, 15 minutes
Service Ceiling: 6,500 feet (2,000 metres)
Rate of Climb: 200 feet per minute (61 metres per minute)

Armament

Guns: None specified

Bristol F.2

Built to replace the Bristol B.E. as a reconnaissance plane, the company's F.2 filled two vital roles: equipped with controls at both pilot and observer seats, wireless radios, and both Vickers and Lewis machine guns, the F.2 was used both for reconnaissance and as a fighter. Experience in combat let the Allies replace the original F.2 engine with a more powerful version. The newly retrofitted F.2, with its superior speed and dive rate, became one of the most successful fighters in the war.

Flown by: None of the aces

General Specifications

Manufacturer: British and Colonial Aeroplane Company
Designer: Frank Barnwell
First Flight: September 9, 1916
Introduced: 1916
Retired: 1930s
Primary User: RFC, Polish Air Force
Number Built: 5,329
Crew: Two (pilot and observer/gunner)
Length: 25 feet, 10 inches (7.87 metres)

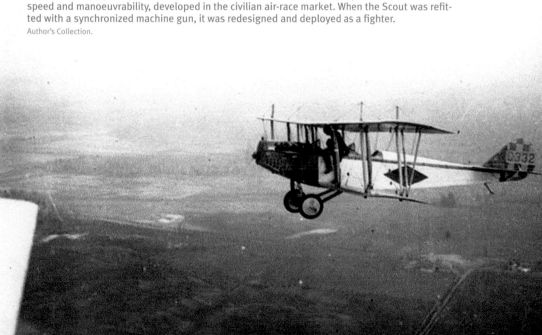

Bristol Scout A. A Bristol Scout A photographed late in the spring of 1914. Originally the Bristol Scout was employed by both the RFC and the RNAS as a reconnaissance plane because of its speed and manoeuvrability, developed in the civilian air-race market. When the Scout was refitted with a synchronized machine gun, it was redesigned and deployed as a fighter.
Author's Collection.

Bristol Fighter at Shuttleworth. After flying the Bristol F.2 Fighter the pilots and crew affectionately rechristened the aircraft as the "Brisfit" or "Biff." It would see service well into the 1930s.

Wingspan: 39 feet, 3 inches (11.96 metres)
Height: 9 feet, 9 inches (2.97 metres)
Wing Area: 405 square feet (37.62 square metres)
Empty Weight: 2,145 pounds (975 kilograms)
Loaded Weight: 3,243 pounds (1,474 kilograms)
Power Plant: 1 × Rolls-Royce Falcon III liquid-cooled V12 engine, 275 horsepower (205 kilowatts)

Performance

Maximum Speed: 123 mph (198 km/h)
Cruise Speed: 110 mph (177 km/h)
Stall Speed: 52 mph (84 km/h)
Range: 369 miles (593 kilometres)
Endurance: 3 hours
Service Ceiling: 18,000 feet (5,500 metres)
Rate of Climb: 889 feet per minute (270 metres per minute)

Armament

Guns: 1 × .303-inch (7.7-millimetre) forward-firing Vickers machine gun; 1 or 2 × .303-inch (7.7-millimetre) Lewis Guns
Bombs: 240 pounds (110 kilograms)

Bristol Scout

When the Royal Flying Corps decided it needed an aircraft capable of high-speed pursuit, it turned to British aircraft designer Frank Barnwell, developer of some of the fastest racing planes in the world. The Scout was fast and handled well, but early versions suffered from a lack of guns. Further, the plane was tiny — even the smallest pilot struggled to get into and out of the Scout's cockpit. The plane became much more lethal when it was armed with Lewis guns. The Scout came into its own as the first Allied plane to be equipped with machine guns that were synchronized to fire through the spinning propeller.

Flown by: MacLaren

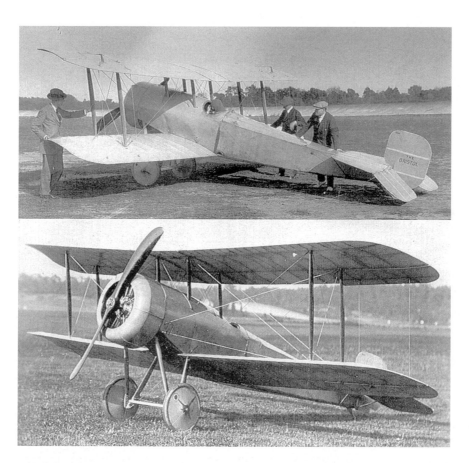

Bristol Scout A. A Bristol Scout A photographed late in the spring of 1914. Originally the Bristol Scout was employed by both the RFC and the RNAS as a reconnaissance plane because of its speed and manoeuvrability, developed in the civilian air-race market. When the Scout was refitted with a synchronized machine gun, it was redesigned and deployed as a fighter.
Author's Collection.

General Specifications

Manufacturer: British and Colonial Aeroplane Company
Designer: Frank Barnwell
First Flight: February 23, 1914
Introduced: 1914
Retired: 1916
Primary User: RFC, RNAS, AFC
Number Built: 374
Crew: One
Length: 20 feet, 8 inches (6.30 metres)
Wingspan: 24 feet, 7 inches (7.49 metres)
Height: 8 feet, 6 inches (2.59 metres)
Wing Area: 198 square feet (18.40 square metres)
Empty Weight: 789 pounds (358 kilograms)
Loaded Weight: 1,195 pounds (542 kilograms)
Power Plant: 1 × Le Rhône 9C rotary piston engine, 80 horsepower
(60 kilowatts)

Performance

Maximum Speed: 94 mph (151 km/h)
Endurance: 2.5 hours
Service Ceiling: 16,000 feet (4,900 metres)
Rate of Climb: 450 feet per minute (137 metres per minute)

Armament

Guns: 1 × Lewis or Vickers machine gun

S.E.5

Nicknamed the "Ace Maker," the S.E.5 was flown by more British aces
than any other aircraft during the First World War. The plane had a powerful engine that delivered both a high top speed and a formidable climb
rate. Known by pilots to be a strong and reliable airplane, the S.E.5 had a
few weaknesses. Because of the power of its engine and the relatively large
wing area, the S.E.5 proved impossible to land at high speed and, if a
pilot forced the matter, the landing gear had a tendency to break off. The
good news for pilots was that the plane handled well at low speeds, which
gave it an advantage against planes that could not match its slower speeds.

S.E.5a, Masterton, New Zealand. Despite its chronic engine problems, the S.E.5 was very popular with pilots because of its high performance capabilities. While the S.E.5 was never built in large numbers, it and the Sopwith Camel ended German air superiority in April 1917 (Bloody April).

Flown by: McCudden, Proctor, McElroy

General Specifications

Manufacturer: Royal Aircraft Factory
Designer: Henry Folland and John Kenworthy
First Flight: November 22, 1916
Introduced: March 1917
Retired: Used past the end of the war for military and civilian purposes
Primary User: RFC, United States Army Air Service
Number Built: 5,205
Crew: One
Length: 20 feet, 11 inches (6.38 metres)
Wingspan: 26 feet, 7 inches (8.11 metres)
Height: 9 feet, 6 inches (2.89 metres)
Wing Area: 244 square feet (22.67 square metres)
Empty Weight: 1,410 pounds (639 kilograms)
Loaded Weight: 1,935 pounds (880 kilograms)
Power Plant: 1 × Hispano-Suiza 8 or Wolseley Viper water-cooled V8 engine, 200 horsepower (150 kilowatts)

Performance

Maximum Speed: 138 mph (222 km/h)
Cruise Speed: 90 mph (145 km/h)
Stall Speed: 56 mph (90 km/h)
Range: 300 miles (483 kilometres)
Endurance: 1 hour, 50 minutes (combat); 3 hours, 50 minutes (cruise)
Service Ceiling: 17,000 feet (5,185 metres)
Rate of Climb: 755 feet per minute (230 metres per minute)

Seventeen British S.E.5as, in Arrow. A long row (seventeen aircraft) of British SE.5as wait to do battle on the Western Front. Author's Collection.

Armament

Guns: 1 x .303-inch (7.7-millimetre) forward-firing Vickers machine gun with Constantinesco interrupter gear; 1 x .303-inch (7.7-millimetre) Lewis gun on Foster mounting on upper wing
Bombs: 4 x 25-pound (11-kilogram) Cooper bombs, two under each lower wing, to be dropped in 2, 3, 4, 1 order.

Nieuport 17

The Nieuport 17 replaced the Nieuport 11, and was one of the most successful fighters on the Allied side. Pilots liked the Nieuport 17's speed and the fact that the plane allowed the pilot great visibility in combat. Well-armed with a Vickers machine gun, and sometimes an additional Lewis gun, the Nieuport was lethal. The plane did have a disconcerting fault: in a high-speed dive, the lower wing was known to collapse and tear away. Only two pilots were ever recorded to have survived the loss of the lower wing on the Nieuport 17.

Flown by: Bishop, McElroy

Nieuport 17. Allied pilots loved the Nieuport 17 for its rapid rate of climb and manoeuvrability. The plane's only downside was that the wings tended to fall off if the pilot flew it into a deep, sustained dive.

Nieuport 17, Front. A French Newport 17 equipped with the Gnome Rotary engine and Chauviere propeller.

Author's Collection.

General Specifications

Manufacturer: Nieuport
First Flight: January 1916
Introduced: March 1916
Retired: Late 1917
Primary User: Aéronautique Militaire
Number Built: 7,200
Crew: One
Length: 19 feet (5.80 metres)
Wingspan: 26 feet, 9 inches (8.16 metres)
Height: 7 feet, 10 inches (2.40 metres)
Wing Area: 158.8 square feet (14.75 square metres)
Empty Weight: 825 pounds (375 kilograms)
Loaded Weight: 1,232 pounds (560 kilograms)
Power Plant: 1 × Le Rhône 9Ja 9-cylinder rotary engine, 110 horse-power (82 kilowatts)

Planes in Line for Inspection, Issoudon, France.
An impressive photo of twenty-six Nieuport
17s in line for inspection at the aviation field
at Issoudon, France, April 1918.
Author's Collection.

Performance

Maximum Speed: 110 mph (177 km/h)
Cruise Speed: 99 mph (160 km/h)
Stall Speed: 40 mph (64 km/h)
Range: 155 miles (250 kilometres)
Endurance: 1.75 hours (combat); 2 hours, 40 minutes (cruise)
Service Ceiling: 17,390 feet (5,300 metres)
Climb: 673 feet per minute (205 metres per minute)

Armament

Guns: 1 × synchronized Vickers machine gun (French service); (British service) 1 × Lewis gun on Foster mounting on upper wing (British service)
Rockets: 8 Le Prieur rockets

B.E.2

The B.E.2 was one of the first military aircraft flown by the Royal Air Force. The plane was perfect as a platform for reconnaissance. Stable and slow, the B.E 2 allowed observers to see clearly what was happening on the ground, so they could provide important intelligence. The difficulty was that the B.E.2 was unarmed, so pilots and observers were often reduced to shooting at the enemy with pistols and rifles. When the German Fokker Eindecker aircraft entered the war in 1915, its forward-firing guns were extremely lethal — and the B.E.2 was easy prey.

Flown by: Barker

General Specifications

Manufacturer: Royal Aircraft Factory, Vickers, Bristol
Designers: Geoffrey de Havilland, E.T. Busk
First Flight: February 1, 1912
Introduced: 1912
Retired: 1919
Primary User: RFC
Number Built: 3,500
Crew: Two (pilot and observer)
Length: 27 feet, 3 inches (8.31 metres)
Wingspan: 37 feet (11.28 metres)

Replica RAF B.E.2c. A replica of the B.E.2. The B.E.2 was used by the Royal Flying Corps as a reconnaissance aircraft and a light bomber from 1912 to the end of the war. In addition, the B.E.2 provided the perfect platform for aerial photography.

Height: 11 feet, 1½ inches (3.39 metres)
Wing Area: 371 square feet (34.8 square metres)
Empty Weight: 1,370 pounds (623 kilograms)
Loaded Weight: 2,350 pounds (1,068 kilograms)
Power Plant: 1 × RAF 1a air-cooled V8 engine, 90 horsepower (67 kilowatts)

Performance

Maximum Speed: 72 mph (116 km/h) at 6,500 feet (1,980 metres)
Cruise Speed: 65 mph (104 km/h)
Stall Speed: 51 mph (82 km/h)
Range: 200 miles (321 kilometres)
Endurance: 3 hours, 15 minutes
Service Ceiling: 10,000 feet (3,050 metres)
Rate of Climb: 1,066 feet per minute (324 metres per minute)

Armament

Guns: 1 × .303-inch (7.7-millimetre) Lewis gun for observer
Bombs: 224 pounds (100 kilograms)

R.E.8

The R.E.8 was built to replace the B.E.2. The new design moved the pilot to the front, instead of behind the observer, as in the B.E.2. This change allowed for both a forward-firing machine gun for the pilot and a rear-facing machine gun operated by the observer. While the new guns were welcomed by the pilots and observers, the plane was not easy to handle. If the pilot made the smallest error, it could put the plane into a deadly spiral downward. Even the guns became a liability: if the rear-facing observer was not careful, he could inadvertently shoot off the tail of his own plane. Despite its shortcomings, the R.E.8 came to be trusted by the crews and it was the most popular British two-seat aircraft in the war.

Flown by: Barker

General Specifications

Manufacturer: Royal Aircraft Factory
Designer: John Kenworthy
First Flight: June 17, 1916
Introduced: 1916
Retired: 1918
Primary User: RFC
Number Built: 4,077
Crew: Two (pilot and observer/gunner)
Length: 27 feet, 10½ inches (8.50 metres)
Wingspan: 42 feet, 7 inches (12.98 metres)
Height: 11 feet, 4½ inches (3.47 metres)
Wing Area: 377.5 square feet (35.1 square metres)

Royal Aircraft Factory R.E.8. The R.E.8 was built by the Royal Aircraft Factory as a reconnaissance aircraft and bomber. The R.E.8 replaced the B.E.2, but pilots complained that the new plane was much more difficult to handle and manoeuvre.

Empty Weight: 1,803 pounds (820 kilograms)
Loaded Weight: 2,678 pounds (1,217 kilograms)
Power Plant: 1 × Royal Aircraft Factory 4a air-cooled V12 engine, 140 horsepower (104 kilowatts)

Performance

Maximum Speed: 103 mph (166 km/h)
Cruise Speed: 102 mph (165 km/h)
Stall Speed: 47 mph (76 km/h)
Range: 373 miles (600 kilometres)
Endurance: 4 hours, 15 minutes
Service Ceiling: 13,500 feet (4,115 metres)
Rate of Climb: 300 feet per minute (91 metres per minute)

Armament

Guns: 1 x .303-inch (7.7-millimetre) forward-firing Vickers gun; 1 or 2 x .303-inch (7.7-millimetre) Lewis guns in rear cockpit
Bombs: up to 224 pounds (102 kilograms)

R.E.8 Cockpit Area. The R.E.8 was used by Allied air forces throughout the First World War on the Western Front, in Italy, in Russia, in Palestine, and in Mesopotamia. Before flights, it was common for intelligence officers to meet and brief the crews of departing R.E.8s.
Author's Collection.

Airco DH.4

The Airco DH.4 filled the role of a light, two-seat bomber for the Allies late in the war. Armed with a forward-firing Vickers machine gun and rear-facing Lewis guns, and with high speed, manoeuvrability, and a high altitude ceiling, the plane often flew without fighter protection. The only complaint crews had about the plane was that the position of the fuel tank between the pilot and observer often made communication difficult.

Flown by: None of the aces

General Specifications

Manufacturer: Airco
Designer: Geoffrey de Havilland
First Flight: August 1916
Introduced: March 1917
Retired: 1932
Primary User: RFC, United States
Number Built: 1,449 in the UK, 4,846 in the U.S.
Crew: Two
Length: 30 feet, 8 inches (9.35 metres)
Wingspan: 43 feet, 4 inches (13.21 metres)
Height: 11 feet (3.35 metres)
Wing Area: 434 square feet (40 square metres)
Empty Weight: 2,387 pounds (1,085 kilograms)
Loaded Weight: 3,472 pounds (1,578 kilograms)
Power Plant: 1 × Rolls-Royce Eagle VII inline liquid-cooled piston, 375 horsepower (289 kilowatts)

Performance

Maximum Speed: 143 mph (230 km/h)
Cruise Speed: 90 mph (145 km/h)
Range: 470 miles (770 kilometres)
Endurance: 3 hours
Service Ceiling: 22,000 feet (6,700 metres)
Rate of Climb: 1,000 feet per minute (305 metres per minute)

FRANCE
1918

Airco DH.4. An Airco DH.4 flies high above the clouds in France. The DH.4 was originally designed as a bomber for daytime operations, but many fighter pilots and future aces would learn their flying skills at the stick of the DH.4.
U.S. Library of Congress.

DE HAVILAND
"4"

Armament

Guns: Forward-firing .303-inch (7.7-millimetre) Vickers machine gun; Lewis gun on Scarff ring at rear
Bombs: 460 pounds (210 kilograms)

Avro 504

On November 21, 1914, three Avro 504 bombers staged the first organized bombing raid in history. Flying together, the three RNAS 504s targeted and hit the sheds housing airships at Freidrichshafen, Germany. Build specifically as a bomber and reconnaissance plane, the 504 served successfully throughout the First World War, including as a trainer for new bomber crews.

Flown by: Bishop

General Specifications

Manufacturer: Avro
First Flight: September 18, 1913
Introduced: 1913
Retired: 1932

1913 Wars of the Roses, Doncaster Control. In a pre-war photo, a Blackburn Type 1 and an Avro 504 (right) line up for the start of the Wars of the Roses air race. The Avro 504 was one of the most common aircraft on the battlefield of the First World War: 8,970 were built for Allied use by the end of the war, and 10,000 more after the war's end.
Author's Collection.

Primary Users: RFC, RNAS
Number Built: 8,970
Crew: Two
Length: 29 feet, 5 inches (8.97 metres)
Wingspan: 36 feet (10.97 metres)
Height: 10 feet, 5 inches (3.18 metres)
Wing Area: 330 square feet (30.7 square metres)
Empty Weight: 1,231 pounds (558 kilograms)
Loaded Weight: 1,829 pounds (830 kilograms)
Power Plant: 1 × Le Rhône Rotary, 110 horsepower (82 kilowatts)

Performance

Maximum Speed: 90 mph(145 km/h)
Cruise Speed: 75 mph (121 km/h)
Stall Speed: 43 mph (69 km/h)
Range: 250 miles (402 kilometres)
Endurance: 3 hours
Service Ceiling: 16,000 feet (4,876 metres)
Rate of Climb: 700 feet per minute (213 metres per minute)

Armament

Guns: Lewis machine gun in forward mount

German Airplanes

Albatros D.V

The Albatros D.V was designed as the German answer to the fighter planes the Allies were putting in the air in the spring of 1917. The pilots that flew the D.V liked the airplane for its speed, manoeuvrability, and ability to maintain high altitudes. However, like the Allied Nieuport 17, the D.V had a tendency to lose its lower wings in a high-speed dive. Because of this, the German pilots were always careful not to push their D.Vs too hard.

Flown by: Ernst Udet

General Specifications

Manufacturer: Albatros-Flugzeugwerke
First Flight: April 1917
Introduced: April 1917
Retired: 1918
Primary User: Luftstreitkräfte
Number Built: 2,500
Crew: One
Length: 24 feet, 1 inch (7.33 metres)
Wingspan: 29 feet, 8 inches (9.05 metres)
Height: 8 feet, 10 inches (2.7 metres)
Wing Area: 228 square feet (21.2 square metres)
Empty Weight: 1,515 pounds (687 kilograms)
Loaded Weight: 2,066 pounds (937 kilograms)
Power Plant: 1 × Mercedes D.IIIaü piston engine, 200 horsepower
(150 kilowatts)

Performance

Maximum Speed: 116 mph (186 km/h)
Cruise Speed: 98 mph (157 km/h)

German Planes at Huj, First World War. German Albatross D.III fighters from Flieger Abteilung 300 on the airfield at Huj, 9.6 miles (15 kilometres) north-east of Gaza.

Albatros D.Va. Approximately 900 D.V and 1,612 D.Va airplanes were built for the German military. While the planes would stay in service until the end of the war, production officially ended in early 1918.

Stall Speed: 50 mph (80 km/h)
Range: 217 miles (350 kilometres)
Endurance: 1 hour, 30 minutes (combat); 3 hours 10 minutes (cruise)
Service Ceiling: 18,701 feet (5,700 metres)
Rate of Climb: 821 feet per minute (250 metres per minute)

Armament

Guns: 2 × .312-inch (7.9-millimetre) LMG 08/15 machine guns

Fokker E.II

On June 13, 1915, Crown Prince Wilhelm of Germany and a group of German commanders watched as the Fokker E.II took its first flight. The plane, unlike its predecessor the E.I, was purpose-built for the battlefield, having an integrated weapons system on board. By the end of June, the E.II was already providing combat victories for German pilots.

Flown by: None of the aces

Fokker E.II of Feldflieger Abteilung 14, Landing.
Fokker E.II 35/15 from Feldflieger Abteilung 14, landing at an airfield on the Eastern Front. With only forty-nine E.IIs built and forty-five serving on the Western Front, it was very unusual to see the aircraft in the East. Sitting on the ground is a Rumple aircraft.

General Specifications

Manufacturer: Fokker-Flugzeugwerke
Designer: Anthony Fokker
First Flight: June 13, 1915
Introduced: June 1915
Retired: 1915
Primary User: Luftstreitkräfte
Number Built: 49
Crew: One
Length: 23 feet, 7 inches (7.2 metres)
Wingspan: 31 feet, 10 inches (9.7 metres)
Height: 9 feet, 2 inches (2.8 metres)
Wing Area: 170 square feet (16 square metres)
Empty Weight: 750 pounds (340 kilograms)
Loaded Weight: 1,102 pounds (500 kilograms)
Power Plant: 1 × Oberursel U.I 9-cylinder air-cooled rotary engine, 101 horsepower (75 kilowatts)

Performance

Maximum Speed: 87 mph (140 km/h)
Range: 123 miles (198 kilometres)

Endurance: 1 hour, 30 minutes
Service Ceiling: 11,811 feet (3,600 metres)
Rate of Climb: 328 feet per minute (100 metres per minute)

Armament

Guns: 1 × forward-firing .312-inch (7.9-millimetre) Maschinengewehr 08 machine gun

Fokker E.III

Unlike the more familiar biplanes and triplanes flown by both sides in the First World War, the Fokker E.III was a monoplane. In addition to its unique design, the E.III was distinguished by being the first aircraft in the war to have a system that synchronized the propeller and the plane's machine guns, allowing the pilot to shoot through the propeller as it spun. The innovation gave the E.III a huge advantage in a dogfight. Allied pilots called the plane the "Fokker Scourge," while nicknaming their own planes "Fokker Fodder."

Flown by: Udet, Jacobs

General Specifications

Manufacturer: Fokker-Flugzeugwerke
Designer: Anthony Fokker
First Flight: 1915
Introduced: December 1915
Retired: 1916
Primary User: Luftstreitkräfte
Number Built: 249
Crew: One
Length: 23 feet, 7 inches (7.2 metres)
Wingspan: 31 feet, 3 inches (9.52 metres)
Height: 7 feet, 10 inches (2.4 metres)
Wing Area: 170 square feet (16 square metres)
Empty Weight: 880 pounds (399 kilograms)
Loaded Weight: 1,345 pounds (610 kilograms)
Power Plant: 1 × Oberursel U.I 9-cylinder rotary engine, 100 horsepower (75 kilowatts)

Performance

Maximum Speed: 87 mph (140 km/h)
Cruise Speed: 54 mph (87 km/h)
Range: 223 miles (359 kilometres)
Endurance: 3 hours (combat or cruise)
Service Ceiling: 11,810 feet (3,600 metres)
Rate of Climb: 656 feet per minute (200 metres per minute)

Armament

Guns: 1 × .312-inch (7.9-millimetre) LMG 08/15 machine gun offset to starboard, synchronized to fire through the propeller.

Fokker D.II

The Fokker D.II, a single-seat fighter, was built to replace the German monoplanes that were quickly falling behind the Allied aircraft they were facing. Introduced in June 1916, the plane responded well, especially when flown by the, by then, very experienced German pilots. However, technology and combat techniques were changing quickly, and the D.II was removed from service only six months later to be replaced by newer, more advanced planes.

Flown By: Jacobs

General Specifications

Manufacturer: Fokker Flugzeugwerke
Designer: Marten Kreutzer
First Flight: 1916
Introduced: 1916
Primary User: Germany
Number Built: 177
Crew: One
Length: 21 feet (6.40 metres)
Wingspan: 28 feet, 9 inches (8.75 metres)
Height: 8 feet, 4 inches (2.55 metres)
Wing Area: 194 square feet (18 square metres)
Empty Weight: 847 pounds (384 kilograms)
Loaded Weight: 1,268 pounds (575 kilograms)

Power Plant: 1 × Oberursel U.I rotary, 100 horsepower (75 kilowatts)

Performance

Maximum Speed: 93 mph (150 km/h)
Cruise Speed: 76 mph (123 km/h)
Range: 124 miles (200 kilometres)
Endurance: 1.5 hours
Service Ceiling: 13,125 feet (4,000 metres)
Rate of Climb: 820 feet per minute (249 metres per minute)

Armament

Guns: 1 × fixed, forward-firing .312-inch (7.9-millimetre) IMG 08 machine gun

Fokker DR.I

If there is a single First World War airplane that is recognized by almost everyone. it is the Fokker DR.I. The DR.I is most associated with Manfred

Fokker DR.I Triplane. The Fokker DR.I Dreidecker (triplane) was designed to answer the threat of the Allies' Sopwith Camel on the Western Front in 1917. The Camel could outmanoeuvre the German Albatros, but the DR.I could match the Camel turn for turn.

LEFT: Replica Fokker DR.I. Replica Fokker DR.I parked on the grass flight line.
RIGHT: Fokker DR.I Triplane. A replica Fokker DR.I takes to the air over England.

von Richthofen. The German ace used the plane to shoot down nineteen enemy fighters, and he was flying the tri-wing plane when he himself was shot down. For German pilots on the Western Front, the DR.I's speed and manoeuvrability gave them a fighting chance against the Allied Sopwith Camel and Triplane. Even the hyper-critical Red Baron declared it "superior to all foes."

Flown by: Jacobs, Richthofen, Voss

General Specifications

Manufacturer: Fokker-Flugzeugwerke
Designer: Reinhold Platz
First Flight: July 5, 1917
Introduced: 1917
Retired: 1918
Primary User: Luftstreitkräfte
Number Built: 320
Crew: One
Length: 18 feet, 11 inches (5.77 metres)
Wingspan: 23 feet, 7 inches (7.20 metres)
Height: 9 feet, 8 inches (2.95 metres)
Wing Area: 201 square feet (18.7 square metres)
Empty Weight: 895 pounds (406 kilograms)
Loaded Weight: 1,292 pounds (586 kilograms)
Power Plant: 1 × Oberursel Ur.II 9-cylinder rotary engine, 82 kilowatts (110 horsepower)

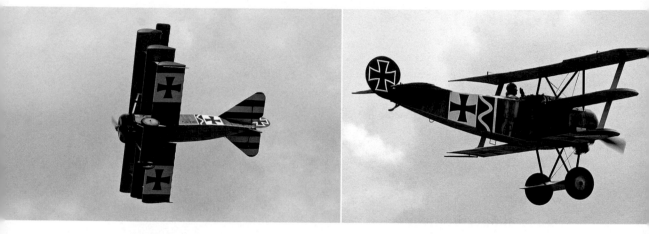

LEFT: **Replica Fokker DR.I.** Manfred von Richthofen (the Red Baron) would fly the DR.I in the last part of his career, shooting down twenty Allied planes in the DR.I until he was killed in the plane by a shot from the ground.
RIGHT: **Replica Fokker DR.I.**

Performance

Maximum Speed: 115 mph (185 km/h)
Cruise Speed: 95 mph (152 km/h)
Stall Speed: 45 mph (72 km/h)
Range: 185 miles (300 kilometres)
Endurance: 1 hour, 40 minutes (combat); 2 hours, 30 minutes (cruise)
Service Ceiling: 20,000 feet (6,095 metres)
Rate of Climb: 1,130 feet per minute (344 metres per minute)

Armament

Guns: 2 × .312-inch (7.9-millimetre) "Spandau" lMG 08 machine guns.

Replica Fokker DR.I, Red Baron Colours. A replica DR.I, painted in the Red Baron's colours, at an airshow.

Aviatik C.I

The Aviatik C.I entered military service as a reconnaissance aircraft in 1915. With the observer, armed with a MG14 machine gun, sitting in front of the pilot, the plane had a limited field of fire. However, with an aggressive crew, the plane could take the offensive facing enemy aircraft. In later models the observer and pilot positions were switched, allowing the rear gunner an even larger field of fire.

Flown by: None of the aces

General Specifications

Manufacturer: Aviatik
First Flight: 1915
Introduced: 1915
Retired: 1917
Primary User: Luftstreitkräfte
Number Built: Approx 70
Crew: Two
Length: 26 feet (7.93 metres)
Wingspan: 41 feet, $\frac{1}{4}$ inches (12.5 metres)
Height: 9 feet, $8\frac{1}{8}$ inches (2.95 metres)
Wing Area: 465.4 square feet (43 square metres)
Empty Weight: 1,650 pounds (750 kilograms)
Loaded Weight: 2,948 pounds (1,340 kilograms)

Aviatik. In Namibia (then German Southwest Africa), a Aviatik C is prepared for flight. In early versions of the aircraft, the observer sat in front of the pilot, partially blocking his view; later versions would have the two switching places.

Power Plant: 1 × Mercedes D III 6-cylinder water-cooled inches-line, 160 horsepower (119 kilowatts)

Performance

Maximum Speed: 88.75 mph (142 km/h)
Stall Speed: 49 mph (79 km/h)
Endurance: 3 hours
Service Ceiling: 3,500 metres (11,500 feet)
Rate of Climb: 254 feet per minute (77 metres per minute)

Armament

Guns: 1 machine gun in rear cockpit

Fokker DV.III

When the German High Command called for a new aircraft in 1918, the Fokker Company responded with the DV.III. The airplane was chosen as the best overall fighter at the Second Fighter Competition in May 1918, and was in full production by August of that year. Despite its success at the Competition, in combat the DV.III had a fatal flaw in its wing design, and almost immediately German pilots were crashing and dying in the plane. By October 1918, it was determined that Fokker had used both poor construction techniques and poor materials in manufacturing the plane. It didn't matter — the First World War ended on November 11, 1918.

Flown by: Löwenhardt

General Specifications

Manufacturer: Fokker-Flugzeugwerke
Designer: Reinhold Platz
First Flight: May 1918
Introduced: May 1918
Retired: 1918
Primary User: Luftstreitkräfte
Number Built: 381
Crew: One
Length: 19 feet, 3 inches (5.86 metres)
Wingspan: 27 feet, 4 inches (8.34 metres)

LEFT: Museum Stamp, Fokker DV.III. The Fokker D.VIII had the distinction of scoring the last victory in the air in the First World War. Introduced as the Fokker E.V late in the war, the plane suffered multiple crashes due to poor design. A new model, the DV.III, reduced the design flaws and dramatically increased the effectiveness of the plane.

RIGHT: American SPADs in Tent Hangar. American SPAD aircraft are repaired in a tent hangar, somewhere on the battlefield.
Author's Collection.

Height: 8 feet, 6 inches (2.6 metres)
Wing Area: 115 square feet (10.7 square metres)
Empty Weight: 893 pounds (405 kilograms)
Loaded Weight: 1,334 pounds (605 kilograms)
Power Plant: 1 × Oberursel UR.II 9-cylinder air-cooled rotary piston engine, 110 horsepower (82 kilowatts)

Performance

Maximum Speed: 127 mph (204 km/h)
Cruise Speed: 100 mph (167 km/h)
Range: 175 miles (282 kilometres)
Endurance: 1 hour, 30 minutes (combat); 2 hours, 30 minutes (cruise)
Service Ceiling: 19,685 feet (6,000 metres)
Rate of Climb: 1,640.4 feet per minute (500 metres per minute)

Armament

Guns: 2 × .312-inch (7.9-millimetre) "Spandau" MG 08 machine guns

LEFT: British Plane in the Air Over Fields. Close up of a British plane flying low over the fields of Flanders.
Author's Collection.
RIGHT: German Plane in the Air over Town. The view from a German aircraft as it circles a town, circa 1918.
Author's Collection.

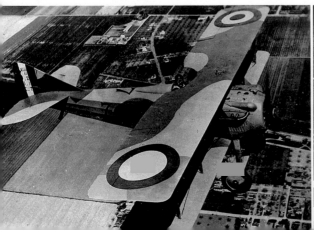

SEVEN

The Iconic Dogfights

December 19, 1915: Malcolm McBean Bell-Irving becomes the first Canadian pilot to shoot down an enemy plane in the First World War.

In the days before machine guns were mounted on aircraft, pilots fired at each other with shotguns and revolvers. Malcolm McBean Bell-Irving once tried to shoot a German pilot with a revolver. When the gun misfired, Bell-Irving threw the revolver at the German and it hit him in the head. Both men survived.

From the very beginning of the war, pilots and commanders alike saw the value of aircraft in combat. It was clear that aircraft would be useful in surveillance and bombing, as their speed and altitude provided a tactical advantage over the enemy stuck on the ground.

The bigger question was how planes could engage each other in combat. There was a need for a way to destroy the bombers and reconnaissance planes flying over the battlefield. As planes flew higher and higher, ground fire became less and less effective.

The answer was the fighter. The plan was to use light, fast aircraft to pursue and shoot down the enemy planes. The challenge was how to arm the planes and what tactics to use. No one had the answers — yet. The first pilots took personal arms, sometimes hunting guns they brought from home to the front, with them in their planes. Quickly, tactics evolved, and mounted machine guns replaced revolvers and shotguns.

Soon, fighter planes on both sides of the conflict were no longer simply chasing slow bombers and unarmed reconnaissance planes. Now they were protecting those planes from other fighters. The dogfight had been invented. As new methods of air-to-air combat were developed, the dogfight grew from one-on-one fights to scenes of multiple aircraft twisting and turning over the battlefield, trying to gain advantage — and to destroy one another.

It was in the dogfights of the First World War that the image of the daring pilot was born.

Three Victoria Crosses

There is no higher award in the Empire than the Victoria Cross (VC). When a pilot was awarded the Victoria Cross, the citation was published in the *London Gazette*. Often cryptic and to the point, the citations seldom caught the emotion the pilots felt in combat.

Fokker D.VII Fighter Flying a Loop. A Fokker D.VII flying a loop, circa 1918. The loop was perfected by First World War pilots on both sides of the conflict. The manoeuvre allowed the hunted to become the hunter by ending up behind the enemy.

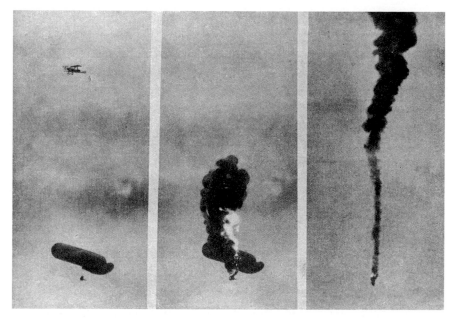

Angriff auf feindlichen Fesselballon, **1918.** Appearing in a German magazine in 1918, this series of photos shows a German biplane attacking and destroying a tethered "kite" observation balloon.

Billy Bishop

The citation for Bishop's Victoria Cross was published in the *London Gazette* on August 11, 1917, and chronicled his solo attack on an enemy aerodrome.

On June 2, 1917, Canadian ace William "Billy" Bishop was flying by himself looking for enemy targets. While pilots often flew together to give each other protection, and a better chance of success, it was not unusual for pilots on both sides to fly solo looking for targets of opportunity. In this case Bishop had asked another pilot, Willy Fry, to be his wingman but the pilot was hungover from a party the night before and declined the invitation.

Bishop first found an enemy aerodrome, but as he circled lower it was clear the field had been abandoned as there were no airplanes or soldiers in sight. No targets or glory to be found.

Continuing his search Bishop decided, despite the dangers, to fly deep over enemy territory. Twelve miles behind enemy lines he spotted another aerodrome. It was Estrourmel the base of Jadgstaffel 5 commanded by Staffel Fuhrer Lt. Werner Voss. On the ground were seven enemy aircraft warming up on the runway.

Bishop immediately attacked. He dove downward, levelling his plane off just 50 feet above the ground. Squeezing the triggers Bishop strafed the waiting aircraft with his machine guns, emptying a 97-round magazine. As he pulled his plane up some of the enemy planes were damaged and a mechanic working at the aerodrome was dead.

Despite Bishop's attack one of the enemy pilots managed to get his Albatros airborne hoping to drive off the Canadian. Bishop quickly wheeled his plane around and, firing fifteen rounds at close range, shot the German down. The plane never got more than sixty feet off the ground.

Another German pilot used the distraction to get his plane in the air. Bishop saw it and, from 150 yards (137.16 metres) away, downed the plane with thirty well-placed rounds. The plane crashed into a tree and lodged itself in the branches hanging precariously above the airfield.

Behind Bishop two other enemy fighters had managed to lift off and were trying to gain as much altitude as possible. If they could get above the Canadian, and attack, the advantage would be theirs. Bishop focussed on one of the planes and chased it to a height of 1,000 feet before he was close enough to engage the enemy pilot. Again, Bishop fired his machine guns — this time emptying a complete drum of ammunition into the enemy. The German plane plummeted to earth.

The final enemy pilot tried to shoot down Bishop while the Canadian was distracted. Bishop saw him and quickly let loose with a stream of bullets. The German pilot broke off, his plane apparently damaged. Bishop used the opportunity to head for his base — with three enemy aircraft to his credit and potentially a fourth.

Farman Wreck. A destroyed Allied Farman aircraft is inspected by German soldiers after the plane was shot down behind enemy lines.

German Plane Brought Down in the Argonne. The remains of a German C.L.IIIa that was shot down by American machine gunners firing from the ground. The plane has red crosses painted on the underside of the wings and the fuselage. The crash occurred in the Argonne between Montfaucon and Cierges, France.

John Warwick Brooke Spotting a German Plane. While the image of two enemy aircraft engaged in combat — the dogfight — is iconic to the First World War, it was often ground fire that proved deadly to pilots on both sides. Many pilots, absorbed with chasing the enemy, would stay close to the ground, becoming relatively large and slow-moving targets. Armed with a Vickers machine gun, a French gunner aims at a distant aircraft with the help of a spotter.

Low on fuel and ammunition, and with one of his guns jammed, Bishop knew he could not fight any more that day. So it was with some nervousness that he noted four enemy fighters flying high overhead, apparently following him.

To avoid being seen he hugged the ground — flying as low as he could. While he avoided the fighters his low altitude made him vulnerable to enemy troops firing from the ground trying to down his plane.

When he landed at Filescamp Aerodrome at 5:40 a.m. he held up three fingers to indicate to the gather ground crew that he had made three kills. The mechanics later discover his plane had a total of seventeen bullet holes in it. It was amazing the Nieuport had been able to fly at all.

James McCudden

The *London Gazette* of April 2, 1918, recorded that Captain James McCudden had been awarded the Victoria Cross. Unlike Bishop, he did not receive the highest award for bravery for one action but as recognition of his overall record.

When McCudden received his Victoria Cross he had already shot down fifty-four enemy aircraft including nineteen over British lines. His credits included having twice, on one day, shot down four enemy aircraft — one set of four in less than ninety minutes.

On the morning of December 23, 1917, McCudden was patrolling over enemy lines and encountered four enemy aircraft. He immediately attacked all four planes and within moments downed two and drove the other deep into German territory.

Short on fuel and ammunition, McCudden turned his plane back to his base where he landed and turned the craft over to the mechanics to refuel and rearm.

Later in the afternoon, on the same day, when the plane was ready, McCudden climbed in and took to the air at the head of his patrol. Almost immediately eight enemy planes attacked and McCudden again downed two.

Just over a month later on January 30, 1918, McCudden again defeated multiple enemy planes by himself. Flying alone he was attacked by five enemy scout aircraft. Throwing his aircraft into the dogfight he managed to shoot down two of the German planes and pushed the rest far to the east and away from McCudden's home base.

Albatros D.III Wreck. Wreck of a German Albatros D.III fighter in Flanders, 1917. In the days before modern communication, verifying the results of a crash was difficult. If a squadron was not sure what had happened to one of its flyers, a single plane would fly over an enemy airfield and drop a streamer with a note attached, asking for details. If an answer was possible, it was delivered in the same way.

Battle of the Triplanes. Two replica triplanes, at a modern airshow in England, engage in mock combat. During the First World War, if a pilot or group of pilots felt an opponent had fought and died well, a lone aircraft would fly over the dead man's airfield and drop a wreath of condolence. By tradition, no one on the ground would fire at the low-flying aircraft.

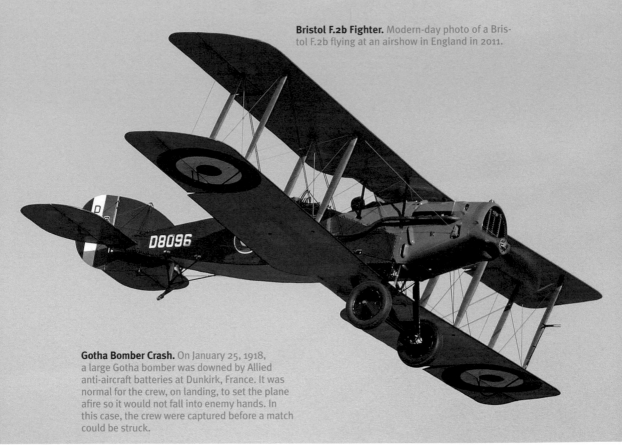

Bristol F.2b Fighter. Modern-day photo of a Bristol F.2b flying at an airshow in England in 2011.

Gotha Bomber Crash. On January 25, 1918, a large Gotha bomber was downed by Allied anti-aircraft batteries at Dunkirk, France. It was normal for the crew, on landing, to set the plane afire so it would not fall into enemy hands. In this case, the crew were captured before a match could be struck.

Replica Fokker DR.I and Nieuport Scout. A replica German DR.I triplane chases a replica Nieuport Scout during a mock dogfight. During the spring of 1917, German aviators were shooting down Allied planes at a ratio of 5 to 1.

When McCudden's plane rolled to a stop at the Allied aerodrome it was discovered that one machine gun was out of ammunition and the other inoperable. Skill, and luck, had been on McCudden's side.

William Barker

On November 30, 1918, the *London Gazette* announced that William Barker had been awarded the Victoria Cross.

William Barker, the Canadian ace, was flying over the Foret de Mormal on the morning of October 27, 1918, when, in front of him, he spotted an enemy plane. Closing on the aircraft he squeezed the trigger on his

DFW Banking. A DFW C.V (Aviatik) airplane banks hard to the left, early in the morning. Shot from another airplane, the photo clearly shows three flares locked in a rack behind the observer and a LMG 14 Parabellum machine gun.

Pilot and Observer, Bristol Aircraft. On the ground in Palestine — air combat was not limited to the Western Front. In this 1918 photo, a pilot (left) of No. 1 Squadron of the Australian Flying Corps consults with his observer.

machine gun and sent the plane plummeting to the ground with a quick, clean burst of fire.

The dogfight had not gone unnoticed. Enemy fighters in the area saw their comrade spiralling down and flew to his assistance. As they swarmed around Barker a Fokker biplane fired on Barker and a bullet tore into the Canadian's right thigh.

Fighting through the pain Barker pulled his plane around and, lining up on the German plane, fired his own guns, killing the enemy pilot.

There was no respite. A swarm of enemy Fokkers rushed to the attack and Barker was again wounded — this time with a bullet in his left thigh. Trying to ignore the excruciating pain Barker shot down another two enemy aircraft before losing consciousness, his plane out of control.

Before Barker's plane hit the ground the Canadian ace regained consciousness and, fending off an attack from a group of German Fokkers, managed to return to the battle destroying another enemy plane, but this time he was shot in the left elbow and again passed out from the pain.

With his plane out of control Barker was in danger of crashing, but somehow he turned the plane back toward the enemy and attacked another enemy plane destroying it.

Finally, with three severe wounds Barker pulled out of the fight and headed for home. As he did, a formation of enemy fighters intercepted him and he was forced to again fight his way through. Exhausted and in severe pain, Barker finally reached his home base. While his plane crashed on landing Barker survived.

LEFT: Fokker DR.I Guns, Close-Up. The machine guns of a Fokker DR.I
RIGHT: R.E.8 at Night. A night photo of a R.E.8 aircraft of No.3 Squadron Australian Flying Corps preparing to take off.

Fokker DR.I, Inverted. In 1903, the Wright brothers surprised the world by flying a heavier-than-air craft for the first time. Less than fifteen years later, pilots would push the limits of their aircraft, like this Fokker DR.I flying fully inverted.

Death of the Red Baron

The death of Germany's greatest ace, the Red Baron, came at the hands of a Canadian ace — at least, that is what everyone believed.

On April 21, 1918, at 11:00 a.m., Richthofen was flying by Morlancourt Ridge near the River Somme. He soon spotted a Sopwith Camel and gave pursuit. There was no way for the Red Baron to know it, but he was chasing Canadian pilot Wilfred "Wop" May of No. 209 Squadron Royal Air Force, then a newcomer to air combat.

May flew close to the ground with the Baron almost literally on his tail. Concentrating on the Sopwith Camel in front of him, the Baron did not see May's flight commander, Canadian Captain Arthur "Roy" Brown, diving in at very high speed. At the last minute, the Baron spotted Brown and broke off his pursuit of May to chase the now rapidly climbing flight commander.

When it seemed Brown was no longer a threat, Richthofen turned his sights back on May. Suddenly the Baron was hit by a single .303 bullet that pierced his heart and lungs. Brown had returned to the fight.

Bleeding profusely, the Baron put his plane down in a field inside the Australian Imperial Force–controlled sector, near the village of Vaux-sur-Somme in France.

Bristol Fighters. A real photo postcard showing Allied Bristol Fighters in the air. Many postcards of the day were faked, using model aircraft for the shots, as capturing real planes in combat took both skill and luck on the photographer's part. Author's Collection.

Australian soldiers quickly surrounded the downed German fighter. Gunner George Ridgway, one of the first to get to the airplane, later reported, "Richthofen was still alive but died moments later."[23] Sergeant Ted Smout of the Australian Medical Corps added, "Richthofen's last word was *kaput*."[24] According to tradition, the nearest Allied air unit, No. 3 Squadron Australian Flying Corps, claimed the German ace's remains.

As for the Baron's Fokker DR.I, it survived the landing — but not the souvenir hunters who tore it apart in the hope of acquiring a piece of history.

Hotchkiss Anti-Aircraft Gun. Allied soldiers set up an improvised anti-aircraft post using a Hotchkiss light machine gun. Author's Collection.

Lewis Guns, Ground. Allied Lewis gunners take aim on a low-flying enemy aircraft.
Author's Collection.

Brown was officially credited with downing the Red Baron, but later a credible case was made that the Baron might have been killed by ground fire coming from the Austrian lines. There may never be a final answer.

Udet vs. Guynemer

An encounter between German ace Ernst Udet and French ace Georges Guynemer in early 1917 showed that the age of chivalry had transferred from the cavalry to the air.

Udet, who had been serving with *Jasta* 15, wrote about the dogfight. He had been on patrol when he crossed paths with Guynemer at an altitude of 16,000 feet (4,877 metres). Guynemer was a dangerous opponent, with thirty kills to his credit. Udet cautiously entered the battle.

As both men jockeyed for position, their aerobatics brought them closer and closer to each other, until Udet could read the small letters on the side of Guynemer's SPAD S.VII. Backing off, Guynemer fired

Bristol S.E.5 and Junkers CL.I. A German Junkers CL.I passes behind a Bristol AC.5 in mock combat at an airshow.

a burst of gunfire though the German's upper wing. Udet dove and turned to evade more gunfire.

Coming up under Guynemer's plane, Udet knew he had the advantage — and perhaps the victory. The German pilot aimed his guns and fired. Nothing. His guns had jammed. Guynemer, knowing his enemy was now effectively unarmed, waved, broke off the flight, and disappeared over the horizon.

Werner Voss over Poelkapelle

German ace Werner Voss took to the air on the morning of September 23, 1917, and quickly shot down an Airco DH.4. He returned safely to his base, despite his aircraft being severely damaged by Allied gunfire.

Allowing mechanics time to repair his plane, Voss calmly ate a lunch and returned to his plane, ready for another sortie over enemy lines.

Colour Postcard, Dogfight. A First World War postcard shows a German aircraft in flames, crashing rearward, while the victorious Allied pilot breaks off — presumably heading for home. Author's Collection.

Plane in Clouds. Alone, an aircraft patrols the skies over the Western Front. The absence of a wingman highlights the fact that ultimately air combat pitted man against man and that it could be very lonely, indeed.
Author's Collection.

On the British side of the battlefield, RFC ace Captain James McCudden, along with Lieutenant Arthur Rhys-Davids, Captain Keith Muspratt, and three other pilots from No. 56 Squadron, B Flight, were readying their planes to head out over the same piece of no-man's land as Voss. Next to them, C Flight was going through its final preparations as well.

At 5:00 p.m. all the British planes taxied out and were soon airborne, pushing through the clouds at 1,000 feet (304 metres) heading to their patrol altitude of 8,000 feet (2,438 metres). As McCudden passed over the town of Bixschoote, Belgium, he noticed dozens of Allied aircraft to the north, looping and diving over the Battle of Passchendaele that was waging below. All the air activity forced McCudden to lead his squadron lower than he wanted to —

Red Baron, Last Photo. The last photo taken of the Red Baron Manfred von Richthofen. The Baron loved dogs, especially Great Danes, and many photos of the famed ace include dogs of various breeds. The Baron's famed triplane is visible in the background.
Author's Collection.

right into heavy German anti-aircraft fire. Despite the conditions, McCudden quickly located and shot down a German DFW.

Voss took off in his Fokker triplane at 6:05 p.m., followed by two flights of German aircraft. The German ace, in the much faster plane, quickly left his fellow flyers behind. At 6:30 p.m. one of the great dog-fights of the First World War began.

Over the town of Poelkapelle, Belgium, the German planes, still trying to catch up to Voss, were engaged by British Sopwith Camels, SPADs, and Bristol F.2s. As the British pilots fired on the enemy, Voss returned to the fight quickly, locating and strafing Lieutenant Harold Hamersley's S.E.5a. When Lieutenant Robert Chidlaw-Roberts rushed to Hamersly's aid, Voss severely damaged Chidlaw-Roberts's aircraft as well. Both men survived, but they were done for the day and limped home with the rest of No. 60 Squadron.

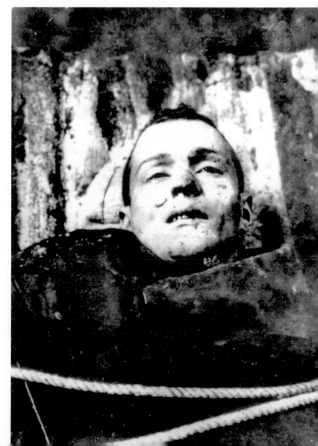

Red Baron, Death Photo. Shot down over Australian lines, probably by a soldier on the ground, the Red Baron died on April 21, 1918. It was originally presumed he was shot down by Canadian pilot Arthur "Roy" Brown, but the angle of the shot through his heart indicated that the Baron had been killed by a lucky shot from the ground.
Author's Collection.

Well-Performed Dogfight. Two replica planes chase each other in mock combat.

It was now McCudden's turn. Together with the other pilots of B Flight, McCudden boxed in Voss with planes. Believing Voss was trapped with nowhere to go, the British planes closed in for the kill.

Voss surprised all of them by putting his plane into a flat spin and, turning in mid-air to face the enemy, becoming the aggressor. Voss fired on Lieutenant Cronyn's S.E.5, quickly damaging it and forcing it to withdraw under cover fire from other planes of B Flight. As Cronyn headed for home, C Flight arrived and joined in the fight.

With British and German planes engaging each other, Voss cut through the enemy planes, never holding a steady course but firing the whole time. Both sides scored victories and suffered losses. Voss seemed to be blessed. At one point, five British planes fired on Voss at the same time — they all missed.

Using his plane's superior flying capabilities Voss took on the remaining six British planes himself. As the planes jostled for position, Voss continued to climb, turn, and dive, all the while firing on and hitting British planes.

However, Voss's luck was quickly running out. As Voss engaged McCudden, his plane was hit from the side. From above, Rhys-Davids fired on the German triplane, raking it from front to back at point-blank range. As Voss turned his plane westward, Rhys-Davids again fired into it; Captain Bowman followed with hits on Voss of his own.

McCudden, flying 3,000 feet (914 metres) above, watched as the German ace hit the ground. The fight had lasted eight minutes. Voss had damaged every British plane he had come up against. At 6:40 p.m., the great German ace was dead at Plum Farm near Frezenberg, Belgium.

Early Dogfights, Fought with Pistol and Rifle. An observer in an Allied plane, early in the war, fires his pistol at the enemy. Before machine guns became regular features, dogfights were very personal duels in the air.
Author's Collection.

EIGHT

After the War

June 3, 1918: An airmail service is inaugurated between Montreal, Quebec City, Boston, and New York City.

June 24, 1918: Captain Brian Peck flies the first official Canadian mail from Montreal to Toronto. The plane is so loaded with cases of liquor that the Curtiss JN-4 cannot fly higher than 39 feet (12 metres).

In 1919 a popular song asked, "How Ya Gonna Keep 'Em Down On the Farm After They've Seen Paree?" For many young men it was a serious question. The war had brought them freedom and adventure and, for some of the survivors, a sense of invulnerability.

The pilots who returned to Great Britain, Canada, and Australia were no different. The excitement of flying in combat could not be replaced by working in a shop or ploughing a field. Many of the former aces sought out adventures in flying circuses, barnstorming shows, or the most dangerous places, including Canada's north.

Billy Bishop

Canadian ace and Victoria Cross recipient William "Billy" Bishop was not ready to leave aviation or the military when the war ended. Bishop travelled throughout North America, lecturing on the methods of air combat he had perfected flying over the trenches of France and Belgium.

As the war faded from memory, so, too, did the need for Bishop's particular brand of expertise. To continue flying, Bishop and fellow Canadian ace William Barker tried their hand at business and established one of Canada's first charter airlines. Named the Bishop and Barker Company, the airline used Martinsyde two-seaters and Curtiss HS2Ls to fly from Toronto Island to the Muskoka cottage country north of Toronto. Unfortunately, the airline was soon hit by legal and financial troubles and, when Bishop suffered a serious air crash, the two friends decided to close the company forever. The aircraft were sold to pay off the company's debts.

Bishop and Barker, still searching for a way to make civilian aviation a paying proposition, agreed to do a barnstorming show at Toronto's Canadian National Exhibition. Putting their war experience to use, the show they put on was very realistic — too realistic. When the pair buzzed low over the crowd, a stampede occurred and some people were injured. Paying for the damages cost the airmen's entire fee. Profit remained elusive.

Toronto from the Air. A shot of Toronto, Canada, from the air, circa 1920.

Despite the setback, Bishop was still well-known, and he parlayed his fame into a civilian career in aviation — not in Canada, but in Great Britain. In 1921 he moved to England and by 1929 he was the chairman of British Airlines. Unfortunately, the Wall Street crash that year and the subsequent world-wide depression wiped out British Airlines and Bishop's personal wealth. After the failure of British Airlines, Bishop returned to Canada, where he was asked to be the vice-president of the McColl-Frontenac Oil Company.

While Bishop had success at the oil company, in 1936 he returned to what he loved — military flying. In January he was appointed as the first Canadian Air Vice-Marshal; by 1939 he was the Air Marshal of the Royal Canadian Air Force, He served throughout the Second World War as Director of Recruiting. Ultimately, Bishop was placed in charge of the British Commonwealth Air Training Plan, which saw more than 167,000 airmen trained in Canada to support the air campaigns in Europe during the Second World War.

Despite his failing health, Bishop went on to form the International Civil Aviation Organization (ICAO), which is still active in Montreal. Bishop finally passed away on September 11, 1956. He was sixty-two years old.

William Barker

With the failure of the Bishop and Barker Company, William Barker joined the CAF in 1920 and was immediately sent to England as a liaison officer. While serving with the British Air Ministry he again worked for a short time with Raymond Collishaw, who was flying for the British in the Middle East.

By 1924 Barker was tired of the bureaucratic life of a liaison officer and was searching out opportunities in Canada. At home the tobacco industry in Ontario was just starting, and Barker saw an opportunity to invest in the new industry. It proved lucrative, but in 1929 Barker suffered a serious case of pneumonia and, not being able to work, was forced to sell his interests to pay his day-to-day bills. When he recovered in the fall of that year, Barker was offered the presidency of the Fairchild Aviation Corporation of Canada, which he accepted in January of 1930.

In March 1930, the Fairchild Company was asked to present a new two-seater aircraft to the Canadian Department of National Defence. Barker, always looking for a chance to fly, climbed into the cockpit to take the plane for a short test run.

As the plane lifted off the runway at the Rockcliffe Aerodrome outside Ottawa, all seemed well. The plane disappeared in the distance, to return

The Flyer. A newly minted civilian aircraft flies in the skies over England.

ten minutes later flying low, hard, and fast. Barker suddenly pulled the plane into a very steep climb. At 200 feet (60 metres), the plane's engine stalled and the aircraft nosedived into the ground. Barker was killed instantly.

Raymond Collishaw

Bishop's friend and fellow ace Raymond Collishaw took a different route at the end of the First World War. He was working on the formation of the Canadian Air Force when the war ended and forced his return to Canada.

In 1918 the White Russians, led by General Denikin, were fighting against the Communists in Siberia. During Operation Michael in March 1918, the German Army had advanced to within 28 miles (40 kilometres) of Paris, so success on the Western Front was far from certain. The Allies were concerned that the collapse of the Tsarist government would allow Germany to move troops from the Eastern Front to the West.

Led by Japan, the Allies committed troops and arms to the Siberian Campaign. Canada and Great Britain were no exception, providing everything from men to aircraft. Raymond Collishaw quickly volunteered to go, as it was the chance to fly in combat again.

Because of his experience in France and Belgium, Collishaw was chosen to command a squadron tasked with supporting the Allied forces on the

Wing Walker. When simply flying was not enough for the crowds, some barnstormers turned to more and more dangerous activities. Here a performer performs a wing walk, to the delight of those watching.
Author's Collection.

ground in Siberia. At first the battles went well. The Communists had little or no air support, and Collishaw and his pilots had the air pretty much to themselves. In one incident, four of Collishaw's Sopwith Camels caught Bolshevik cavalry in the open. The planes broke off the attack only when they ran out of ammunition, leaving behind 1,600 Russian casualties.

The Communists, looking for a way to defeat Allied air power in the region, were soon hiring German pilots, who soon made gains against the Allies.

Despite the best efforts of the Allies, it was clear that the Communists were gaining the upper hand. Abandoning their aircraft, Collishaw and the other Canadians returned to Canada via the Crimea in January 1920. Collishaw finished the Siberian Campaign with one air-to-air kill, downing an

Biplane in Field. Civilian barnstormers flew surplus military aircraft across North America, taking civilians up for rides to experience, no matter for how little time, the excitement of air combat.
Author's Collection.

Albatros D.V. Perhaps more impressive is the fact that he personally dropped a bomb from his Sopwith Camel that sank a target — an enemy gunboat.

Not ready to give up the excitement of flying combat missions, Collishaw fought in Persia (modern-day Iran) and in the Second Italo-Abyssinian War between 1920 and 1936,. In 1939, joining the Allies for the Second World War, he was promoted to Air Commodore and was put in charge of No. 204 Group in North Africa. After fighting for the duration of the Second World War, Collishaw returned home to Canada.

The great First World War ace died on September 28, 1976, in West Vancouver, British Columbia, at the age of eighty-two.

Donald MacLaren

For Donald MacLaren the end of the war in Europe was a time of government cutbacks and reductions. His intention had been to continue serving with the newly established Canadian Air Force but, when he was returned to Canada, he resigned and moved to commercial aviation.

By 1921 MacLaren had established Pacific Airways Limited, with himself as the pilot and a Curtiss HS2L as the only aircraft. His first contracts were for the federal and provincial governments, doing everything from fishery patrols to aerial surveys. As the airline grew, more and more opportunities came its way. In 1928, Pacific Airways merged with Western Canada Airways (WCA) and MacLaren was named Superintendent for

MacLaren and H. Hollick-Kenyon. At the end of the war, Canadian ace Donald MacLaren and H. Hollick-Kenyon flew the first airmail service for WCA between Regina and Moose Jaw, Saskatchewan, and Medicine Hat, Lethbridge, and Calgary, Alberta.

MacLaren after the War. Donald MacLaren became a Canadian folk hero when he founded Pacific Airlines in Canada.

Western Canada. Under his direction, the merged airline was soon flying to the Yukon Territory and other northern destinations.

The airline was still dependent on government contracts to be financially successful, and in 1929 it started the first airmail service between Regina, Moose Jaw, Medicine Hat, Lethbridge, and Calgary. When the Canadian government decided to establish the government-operated national airline Trans-Canada Airlines (TCA) (later to become Air Canada), Western Canada Airlines was financially decimated. Ultimately, WCA was purchased by the Canadian Pacific Railway company and operated as Canadian Pacific Airlines.

For MacLaren the future was at TCA. Over the years, he rose to the rank of Executive Assistant to the President and he retired in 1958. Donald MacLaren, fighter pilot and civil aviation pioneer, passed away in 1989 at the age of ninety-six.

Wop May

While he was not as famous as Bishop or Barker, Wilfred "Wop" May was the Canadian pilot who was being chased by the Red Baron when the German ace met his death. May, before returning to Canada in 1919, became an ace himself.

May's own fame came as a bush pilot who helped open up the Canadian North. The pilot made hundreds of trip to the North in often the most adverse conditions. Many villages in the Northwest Territories knew that the familiar sight of May's airplane meant news from and connection to the outside world to the south.

In January 1929, May made international headlines when he flew his Avro Avian from Edmonton to Fort Vermillion, Alberta, to deliver medicine to the community of Little Red River. The citizens of the tiny village were suffering from an outbreak of diphtheria, and the much-needed medicine on May's plane literally meant the difference between life and death for many.

When May and his fellow pilot Vic Horner, bundled up in fur-lined flight suits, climbed into their open-cockpit airplane, the thermometer was hovering at 20 degrees below zero Fahrenheit (-28 degrees Celsius). Their flight plan took them 267 miles (430 kilometres) to McLennan Lake, where they landed and spent the night. The next day, with the weather even colder, May and Horner once again took to the air, finishing the final 50 miles (80 kilometres) to Fort Vermillion. The medicine arrived just in time to stem the tide of the disease and save the village.

The media quickly grabbed the story of the "race against death," and May and Horner became household names, not just in Canada, but also around the world. May parlayed this fame into a successful company, Commercial Airways, which played a vital role in opening up Canada's North to commercial development. People everywhere were mesmerized by the potential of aircraft to serve a greater good — and not just in wartime.

In 1932 May made headlines again, but this time it was for a manhunt.

Albert Johnson, a loner and a drifter, had settled in the Yukon Territory and built a cabin on the Rat River. Shunning human contact, Johnson set out to make a living for himself by trapping and living off the land. It was not long before he was making enemies, including other fur trappers who accused the man of stealing from their traplines.

When the Royal Canadian Mounted Police (RCMP) tried to serve Johnson with a warrant, the "Mad Trapper" shot and wounded a constable. The RCMP returned fire but Johnson, barricaded in his cabin, refused to surrender. In an effort to dislodge him, the RCMP set the cabin on fire. In the confusion, Johnson escaped.

What ensued was an epic manhunt, with the RCMP chasing Johnson across the roof of the world. During the pursuit Johnson killed another constable and then seemingly disappeared.

Wop May. Wop May, the Canadian the Red Baron was chasing when he met his end, would go on to fame and fortune as a pilot. In the 1930s, May piloted an aircraft in the pursuit of the Mad Trapper of Rat River, a murderer in the Yukon Territory of Canada. It was the first time in the British Empire an aircraft was used to pursue a criminal. Author's Collection.

Across Canada, people followed the chase though live radio broadcasts, their fascination adding to the sense of excitement and desperation. The RCMP decided to try a new tactic, hiring famed aviator Wop May to try to track the fugitive from the air. On February 13, 1932, May was flying above a frozen river when he noticed a set of what appeared to be human tracks breaking out of a deep caribou trail. The fugitive Johnson had been using the caribou tracks to hide his own, but had to leave the river to set up camp for the night.

Turning his plane around, May returned to base and reported his sighting to the Mounties still searching for Johnson on the ground. For the next four days, using May's directions for guidance, the RCMP chased Johnson, drawing ever closer. Finally, on February 17 he was spotted. It was the first time in the British Empire that an airplane figured prominently in solving a crime.

Johnson opened fire on the Mounties. As they scrambled for cover, one of the officers was seriously wounded. However, it was the end for the Mad Trapper. Police bullets tore into him and he collapsed in the snow, dying from his wounds.

May landed his airplane on the icy river just as the last shots were fired. His airplane was quickly commandeered as an air ambulance for the wounded RCMP officer. May flew him 125 miles (201 kilometres) to a doctor who saved the man's life.

After an extended career in civil aviation, Wop May died of a stroke on June 21, 1952, while on vacation.

———

The British, Canadian, and Australian pilots who survived the First World War would go on to change the world forever. Because of them, new territories were discovered and air travel became commonplace. Their pioneering flights led, ultimately, to men landing on the moon.

The combat lessons learned over the fields of Flanders became the core of fighter aircraft tactics still used today. Mannock and von Richthofen laid out scientific methods of fighting in the air that moved away from individual daring and toward teamwork and strategy. Modern flyers are always refining the skills passed down to them. Mannock and Richthofen were inventing the rules as they went along.

Air combat will always depend on the courage of young men and women pushing flying machines to the limit. Those who did not return, killed in the skies above France and Belgium, will be remembered forever as pilots, patriots, and heroes.

Notes

1. Harald Penrose, *British Aviation: The Pioneer Years 1903–1914* (London: Putnam, 1967), 181.
2. Brereton Greenhous and Hugh A. Halliday, *Canada's Air Forces, 1914–1999* (Montreal: Editions Art Global and the Department of National Defence, 1999), 34.
3. "The Fifteen Rules of Mick Mannock," History Learning Site, *www.historylearningsite.co.uk.*
4. Veritas: The Newsletter of the RMC, Issue 19 (2005), *www.rmcclub.ca/eVeritas/2005/Issue019/200519.htm.*
5. William A. Bishop, *Winged Warfare* (New York: George H. Doran Company, 1918).
6. Dan McCaffrey, *Billy Bishop: Canadian Hero* (Toronto: James Lorimer & Company, 1988), 22.
7. Bishop, *Winged Warfare.*
8. *Ibid.*
9. John Norman Harris, *Knights of the Air: Canadian Aces of World War I* (Toronto: MacMillan, 1958), 92–93.
10. George Alexander Drew, *Canada's Fighting Airmen* (MacLean Publishing Company, 1930).
11. Dennis Newton, *Australian Air Aces* (Fyshwyck, Australian Capital Territory: Aerospace Publications, 1996), 45.
12. Norman Franks, *Sopwith Triplane Aces of World War 1* (Oxford: Osprey, 2004), 47.
13. *Ibid.*
14. Mike Rosel, *Unknown Warrior: The Search for Australia's Greatest Ace* (Kew: Arcadia/Australian Scholarly Publishing Ltd., 2012).

15. A.D. Garrisson, *Australian Fighter Aces 1914–1953* (Fairbairn, Australian Capital Territory: Air Power Studies Centre, 1999).

16. Manfred Von Richthofen, *Red Fighter Pilot: The Autobiography of the Red Baron* (St Petersburg, FL: Red and Black Publishers, 2007, reprint).

17. Hayden McAllister, ed., *Flying Stories* (London: Octopus Books, 1982), 54–55.

18. Joachim Castan, *Der Rote Baron: Die ganze Geschichte des Manfred von Richthofen*, (Stuttgart: Klett-Cotta Verlag, 2007).

19. McAllister, *Flying Stories*.

20. Greg VanWyngarden, et al., *Early German Aces of World War I* (Oxford: Osprey Publishing, 2006), 49.

21. Norman Franks, *Fokker DVII Aces of World War 1: Part 1*, Osprey Aircraft of the Aces Vol 53, Greg Vanwyngarden (illustrator) (Oxford: Osprey Publishing, 2003).

22. James McCudden, *Flying Fury: Five Years in the Royal Flying Corps* (Havertown, PA: Casemate, 2009, reprint).

23. Geoffrey Miller, "The Death of Manfred von Richthofen: Who fired the fatal shot?" *Sabretache: Journal and Proceedings of the Military History Society of Australia*, Vol. XXXIX, No. 2.

24. *Unsolved History: Death of the Red Baron*, Discovery Channel, 2002.

Bibliography

Baker, David. *Billy Bishop — The Man and the Aircraft He Flew*. London: Outline Press, 1990.

Barker, Ralph. *The Royal Flying Corps in World War I*. London: Robinson, 2002.

Bishop, Arthur. *True Canadian Heroes in the Air*. Toronto: Prospero, 2004.

Bishop, James. *Social History of the First World War*. London: Angus & Robertson, 1982.

Bishop, William. *The Courage of the Early Morning*. Toronto: McClelland & Stewart, 1965.

Budiansky, Stephen. *Air Power*. London: Viking Press, 2004.

Cacutt, Len. *Great Aircraft of the World*. London: Marshall Cavendish, 1992.

Campbell, Christopher. *Aces and Aircraft of WWI*. London: Treasure Press, 1981.

Ellis, Frank. *Canada's Flying Heritage*. Toronto: University of Toronto Press, 1954.

Gowans, Bruce. *Wings Over Calgary*. Calgary: Historic Society of Alberta, 1990.

Holmes, Richard. *Shots From the Front*. London: Harper Press, 2008.

Mathieson, W.D. *Billy Bishop, VC*. Toronto: Fitzhenry & Whiteside, 1989.

Melady, John. *Pilots — Canadian Stories from the Cockpit*. Toronto: McClelland & Stewart, 1989.

O'Keilly, Elizabeth. *Gentleman Air Ace: The Duncan Bell-Irving Story*. Madeira Park, BC: Harbour Publishing, 1992.

Oppel, Frank. *Early Flight From Balloons to Biplanes*. Secaucus: Castle, 1987.

Ralph, Wayne. *William Barker VC*. Toronto: Wiley and Sons, 2007.

Smith-Matheson, Shirlee. *Maverick in the Sky*. Calgary: Frontenac House, 2007.

Swanston, Alexander. *Atlas of Air Warfare*. London: Amber Books, 2009.

Uttridge, Sarah. *Military Aircraft Visual Encyclopedia*. London: Amber Books, 2009.

Various (dir). *Amazing War Machines* DVD set. Mill Creek Entertainment, 2010.

Various (dir). *Battle for the Skies: The Definitive History of the Royal Air Force* DVD set. Portland, OR: Military Heritage Institute, 2012.

Various (dir). *Victory by Air: A History of the Aerial Assault Vehicle* DVD set. Mill Creek Entertainment: 2010.

Wise, S.F. *Canadian Airmen and the First World War*. Toronto: U of T Press, 1980.